BOSS BRANDING

SEVEN WAYS TO CRAFT A LEGENDARY BRAND STORY

SUDHANA SINGH

Imbue

WHAT READERS SAY

'In this age of wannabe influencers and instant celebrity, now more than ever it is important not to lose visibility of the basic building blocks of a memorable brand. Sudhana strips away all the hubris and takes the reader back to the core principles and tools required for creating a successful brand. Using credible real life case studies with detailed back stories, the book provides ample food for thought for those looking to set out on their own brand building journey.'

'Sudhana Singh certainly has the gravitas and authority to write Boss Branding. Her own brand story is genuine and shows a strong power to follow her destination. She weaves the stories of role models who are passionate and inspirational. I have the pleasure of knowing Masters champion Donald Brown, whose story is skilfully captured: the artist, the sportsman, the motivator. The authenticity of Sudhana's narrative is also a caveat to avoid false friends and fake news, as we follow our dreams to become legendary. A timely book to help all sectors as we rebrand during the COVID crisis.'

'This is an amazing and intricately written story that had me hooked from the start. Even as an experienced marketer it made me question how I approach my goals and how I often forget about my mission, values and delivery. Sudhana Singh's purpose is met. It left me wanting to know how to get more of the magic of the people whose stories are shared. They have it in abundance. Boss Branding has clearly laid out pillars to succeed. It shows that with a few adaptations and razor-sharp focus, we can all become better at exceeding our consumers' needs. The book comes at a testing time for the world and the economy and we have to dig deep and understand more about how we improve our personal brand to reach our goals. An inspirational read Sudhana!'

'Boss Branding is an insightful book full of important information for all entrepreneurs who are keen to establish and position their brands successfully in a competitive market. A must-read during the tumultuous times of the COVID era.'

DEDICATED TO

All of you as you charter your brand story through turbulence.

Mum & Dad, whose quiet heroism plots my story.

My daughters, who brought me the happily ever after.

IN MEMORY OF

My ancestors, whose legacy imbues resilience.

Contents

Introduction

As I write this introduction, the UK, like most of the world, is in lockdown. COVID-19 has thrust us into unprecedented times and created a new norm for life and work. Some global leaders acted swiftly, showing agility as they pivoted to save lives and keep their populations safe. A few were slow to rebrand and clung on to party politics or defensive rhetoric; this opened the door to the beast of poverty that was baying outside. Their actions are writing their brand stories and, no matter what comes after, people will remember how they felt when their leaders took steps to combat the deadly tentacles of this virus.

While COVID-19 crushed the world economy, in the UK, the self-employed and SMEs became the underbelly of the economic collapse. Unlike big business, their rescue packages were slow in coming. In the pre-Coronavirus economy, start-ups, those who were self-employed and SMEs often said that their marketing budget was minuscule - if there was one at all. It was all a bit hit and miss and they didn't know where to start. We don't know what the post-Corona economy will look like but, if the present global science fiction-like scenes are anything to go by, it will take years to recover from the inevitable recession.

A sure-fire way to rebrand in an authentic way is to write your story. And there's no better time to start.

Story branding is both an art and a science. Storytellers meticulously choose words to weave a story. They use skill and experience to craft the plot and themes that capture the imagination of listeners and elicit empathy. The ancient art of oral storytelling around a campfire serves to hand down traditions and culture. Stories define what the audience or villagers stood for. Today, that idea has exploded as the storyteller's audience is a global village. It is recorded, played, read and comes at you from multiple media platforms. But the story is not an end in itself. It is a powerful lever that is applied to the science of branding to influence buying behaviour.

My story began in 1877. My grandad was the eldest of five sons. His parents were slaves. He was more fortunate. His generation broke free of slavery and, at sixteen, he secured his first job as a waiter at a hotel. He woke up at five every day, dressed and then, as the pipe often froze, he washed in icy water that trickled out reluctantly from the tap. He shivered beneath his threadbare coat and tucked his thick curls beneath his cap. His mum handed him freshly-made bread and a mug of hot sweetened tea. He cycled to the hotel in the pitch dark, his only guide, the gleaming frost. Grandad dreamt of owning a little car one day, so his neatly pressed trouser hems didn't get wet in the spiky-cold grass. His meagre wage made a huge impact on the family budget.

Grandad went on to become a serial entrepreneur. He had five very different thriving companies. Public transport was one of them and he ended up owning five buses. He also had a live-in chauffeur. In his spare time, he pursued his first love - sport - and he eventually owned and managed a local football team.

Two generations later, my story shows me constantly breaking free of metaphoric chains. I changed countries and jobs, took risks and pushed the boundaries that were drawn to constrict me, and those that I had inadvertently drawn myself.

Five years ago, I made a career change and started Imbue. I asked my friends for advice. They all had varying degrees of marketing, leadership and life expertise but were unanimous on one thing - I should change my surname. It was not doing me any favours. Every time 'Sudhana Singh' was typed in a search engine, the most dreadful photos and vilification popped up. I sued my previous employers, suffered a miscarriage followed by two successful but life-threatening pregnancies, and endured the breakdown of my marriage. I had severe depression and then PTSD. I published my memoir and it transformed my business, especially with regard to branding, lead generation and leadership coaching. However, there was one certainty as I gave birth to Imbue. I was never going to change my surname. You see, it's my grandad's name and it is part of my brand story.

After my book launch, a colleague rang me and asked who was doing my marketing. She wanted to know how to create a brand story similar to my own. My answer was short and simple. Tell your story; include the failure, humiliation and despair. Because when you do, you have the elements to craft your brand. Following its publication, I gave talks on my story. Once, as I took my place after getting off stage, the man seated next to me said that he didn't have a story. He hadn't experienced any of the things I had, and probably had nothing to share. If this thought has crossed your mind already, you couldn't be more wrong. You do have a story. But there's a way to tell it; and to brand yourself and your company in the process.

In 2019, I had the privilege of being the chair of judges at the UK Business Awards for the Entrepreneur of the Year category. I sat riveted through the finalists' presentations - all of whom were market leaders with impressive turnovers. They walked and talked like entrepreneurial leaders, rose from adversity, practised diversity and took risks that paid off. I began to wonder how I was going to choose between them. Who was I going to award the bronze to, the silver, and the much-coveted gold? But, in the end, my problem was solved when a finalist with a compelling story swayed me.

It was the third indication that brand stories, when done correctly, set you and your business apart.

If you've read the brand stories of legends like Apple, Google and Amazon[1], and wondered how you can find and brand your company without the big marketing budget, this book shows you how. I could have looked at giant global brands, but this has already been done.

Boss Branding crafts the stories of six very ordinary people (just like you and I), who started off with practically nothing. We will co-write the seventh story. At the end of each chapter, I analyse the story plot and offer simple marketing and branding tools to craft your very own boss brand story. There are also questions that help you reflect on your story plot. These are followed by coaching questions that provide scaffolding as you build your brand and find your niche. And then niche again.

The chapters are chronological, allowing you to build the foundation of your story first. The final chapter has two must-haves for your brand story: The Imbue Story Branding Model (ISBM) and the Imbue Story Branding Plan (ISBP).

Ready to brand like a legend? Take your place around the campfire.

Chapter One

The Legend's Voyage

Nine-year-old Graham Hughes was watching his favourite TV programme with his mum. It was Michael Palin's 'Around the World in 80 Days'.

Graham: Did he travel without flying, Mum?

Mum: Yes.

Graham: Has anyone been to every country?

Mum: Yes, there are some people who have.

Graham: But no one has done both at the same time?

Mum: No, son.

Graham: When I grow up, that's what I'm going to do. Visit every country in the world without flying.

Mum: That would take years and years. Besides, it's never been done.

Graham: I will be the first then, Mum. You'll see.

Graham caught the travel bug from his dad who used to pack the family into a camper van and ferry them all over Europe. Even as a youngster, Graham took in more than the sights, food and culture. He began to learn first-hand how locals perceived the way their country was governed. And his other passion – politics - was nurtured. He was in Berlin in the summer of 1990 when the demolition of the Wall began.

When he turned nineteen, he bought a round-the-world ticket and travelled to India, Australia, New Zealand and America. He travelled throughout India without flying; gained confidence and did the same in Australia. It was a wonderful trip, helping him to comprehend how big the world truly was.

ANTICIPATION STAGE

He studied history and politics at university and founded his own company. Liverpool saw many up and coming bands and Graham established himself in the hub of this music scene. He collaborated with other artists, photographers and filmmakers and continued to travel. His then-girlfriend was Australian, and they shared their time between the UK and Australia. Soon, he had travelled to over fifty countries. It was before the YouTube era and he made compilation videos of his travels. The seed that he had planted about travelling the world without flying had taken root. His generation began the conversation about how they should preserve the planet. Graham didn't know it yet, but in his zeal to travel without flying, he started to brand himself as a climate change activist.

He started preparations for his quest. His research confirmed that no one had ever done this. He set his mind on getting into the Guinness Book of Records. YouTube was born and he posted his travel videos. It drew the attention of Lonely Planet who asked if they could use them on their website. He managed to wrangle a meeting at their HQ in Melbourne with David Collins, then Co-founder, who was really interested, if somewhat dubious as to whether it could be done. No one had even attempted it. He asked Graham what made him think it could be achieved. Graham's smiling 'ginger' artist persona with a penchant for madcap adventure, belies the tenacity and shrewd business sense that he was to show over the next four years. He pulled out a dossier with his business plan outlining how to get around the world without flying. This was the result of poring over guidebooks. He had planned most of it meticulously but didn't have a clue as to how he was going to get to the Pacific. He thought he would cross that ocean when he came to it.

He said: I'm doing this anyway. Do you want to come along for the ride?

Instead of: This quest is a life-long dream. Will you pay for it?

Lonely Planet, which was run by the BBC, climbed onboard. They wanted a television show, and National Geographic buckled up too. Graham made up the last 5% of the funding. He was on a shoestring budget.

He also remembered to clarify the rules with Guinness Book of Records:

- No flying.

- No private transport or taxi across an entire continent. A bush taxi was allowed. For example, taxis in Africa where sixteen people would be crammed into a car.

- Step on dry land for a country to be counted.

- Carry a GPS logger while travelling, which logged his position every fifteen seconds.

- Show evidence in the form of passport stamps, video footage and camera stills.

The Dream Stage

In January 2009, he set off by flying to Brazil. Then he took a bus from Buenos Aires and a boat to Uruguay. That was his first official crossing; Graham was exhilarated. Over the next three months, he covered countries in the Americas and the Caribbean. Cuba was tricky because it was designated an official enemy of the US and he wasn't allowed to go there. He applied to the US Treasury department to gain permission to enter but was turned down. He contacted a guy who wrote a book on how to get to Cuba legally, who arranged for him to leave on a boat within 24 hours. Graham was forming his brand with his first slogan: *When one door closes, another opens.* He went on to Canada which, even for a Scouser, was bitterly cold. Except for Belarus, Europe was a visa-free breeze, done in three weeks.

Frustration Stage

Then he headed down into Africa. He always foresaw it as a challenge and thought that it would take a few months. But, a year later, he was still there.

It started with his inability to get a visa for Algeria. He had to get it in London.

So, he went back over to Italy, having travelled across the Mediterranean to the Spanish enclave, north of Morocco and down the west coast of Africa. On the way back from Estonia, he was arrested because they thought he had done a runner from Russia. Thankfully, he was able to prove that he was a European citizen.

But Africa was not done with him. He set out from Morocco on a dusty, hazardous two-day journey through Western Sahara to get a visa at the Mauritanian border. When he arrived at the border point, they informed him that they were not issuing visas. He asked them where he should get the visa from and was told to go 2,000 km back through the Sahara Desert. Which he did. With his Mauritanian visa in hand, he made the journey back to the border. And lo and behold, African bureaucracy now issued visas at the border point. And at a cheaper price!

NIGHTMARE STAGE

He arrived in Senegal and intended to go to Cape Verde Islands. He hired ten Senegalese fishermen to accompany him. They had a pirogue - a wooden canoe - without oars, sails, emergency equipment, GPS or radio. They were miles out at sea for four days and all that stood between them and the seemingly endless expanse of water was their leaky boat. During the night Graham used canvas as a blanket and his life jacket as a pillow. His sleeping bag was drenched. When they arrived in Praia, Graham was charged with smuggling the fisherman into the country. They were interrogated; he tried to explain that he was travelling to every country without flying and had hired the fisherman. They were all thrown into a holding cell at the local police station. It was designed for one person. They slept on the concrete floor and were detained for six days. He recalled that he didn't get the ubiquitous 'one phone call' Hollywood movie style.

However, one of the police officers felt sorry for him and lent him his mobile phone. He called his parents in England, but it rang, and he didn't know if it connected;

all he heard was his voice echoing back at him. He hung up and remembered his brother's number. He sent him a text hoping that he would get it. He did get a call two days later. They managed to get him out.

The fishermen were flown back to Senegal, but Graham had to work out of a way of getting himself out without flying. Every morning he would go to the port and was told that they were leaving the next day. This went on for six weeks. In the end, a German and a Frenchman offered to take him back to Africa.

He said: 'I have so much respect for Greta Thunberg; she's sixteen years old and went back and forth over the Atlantic Ocean on a sailboat. It's insane, absolutely insane. She's amazing; she made the journey in November.'

The next few countries were straightforward. He did have a bit of a problem because many visas were running out but was creative with a blue biro pen.

Two months later he arrived in Congo and it was a problem from the start. He was travelling in a truck and arrived at a checkpoint outside Brazzaville when the police singled him out and went through all his travel tapes. They accused him of spying, shoved him in the back of a car and took him to the police station. They confiscated his phone, camcorder and tapes. After interrogating him he was taken downstairs and left in a room for the day. That evening, they returned his stuff. He Skyped his girlfriend who couldn't believe that he was being held again. He reassured her that he would soon be released. Just then, the door opened, and seven hefty police officers entered. They ripped his mobile phone off him, snatched his glasses and hat, and began to strip him, taking his socks, shoes, t-shirt, jeans and belt. He was frogmarched into a tiny, filthy jail cell which had a moist foam on the floor. He lay there semi-naked, alone and afraid. He woke at dawn covered in mosquito bites. He fumed at the injustice of it all - he had a passport and a visa and was being held without charge. After six days the British Consul rescued him.

However, he always tries to find the funny side of things. They couldn't pronounce his surname correctly and called him Mr Hugs instead of Hughes.

As I listened to his story, even as a resilient native South African, my heart pounded with terror at the thought of an African prison cell. I said he was brave. He replied: 'Not brave - stupid'.

The story was covered on the BBC, and the world began to realise that Graham Hughes was not just a daring hero. He was something else too - a growing legend who was unstoppable. Undaunted, he continued his quest.

His resolve was going to be tested again. This time it was closer to home. And personal. He was in Papua New Guinea when he got the worst possible news from home; his sister had terminal cancer. He flew back to the UK and the family spent the last few heart-breaking weeks of her life together.

He returned to Australia, but the loss hit him hard. He only had seventeen countries left but he just didn't have the fight in him. He felt drained and wanted someone else to take the reins. His mum and dad had been rallying around him, organising everything, getting visas and arranging the long and complicated process of getting him on cargo ships. He was into his third year of travel. The attitude and grit that had got him so far didn't seem enough. Then he recalled his sister's last words to him: 'Don't stop. Don't ever stop because of me.'

He was going to honour her final wish. And did.

On his return to the UK, Guinness Book of Records said that he had entered Russia without a visa and through an unofficial border post. He promptly went to the embassy in London, obtained a £150 visa, hopped on a bus from London to Poland and made it official. Job done.

Later, when South Sudan was granted independence, he visited his final country.

BRANDING VALUES

Graham's travels led him to realise a number of universal truths:

His journey revived his faith in humanity. He found that there are kind people all over the world who will go out of their way to help a stranger in need. He will always be grateful to those who helped him achieve his quest by giving him lifts, letting him sleep on their sofas and putting him in touch with the right people.

He learnt that in this journey, you can't judge people by the actions of their government.

Beneath his smiling exterior, he showed courage in the face of setbacks and very real danger. He visited island countries like Nauru, Maldives and Seychelles, which had pirate-infested waters.

In the beginning, he was very conscious of time, but Africa taught him to kick back and enjoy himself. Things will happen when they happen. He encourages anyone who is contemplating this quest to go for it. The main requirement is the right mindset. However, he issues the caveat that if something looks too good to be true, it probably is. After his African misadventures, he wrote up some travel rules[1], four of which served him well in his life and business:

- Walk with determination, even if you're completely lost.

- Keep a cheery disposition no matter what.

- Trust your gut.

- Always have a back-up plan.

While he never took himself too seriously, he has laser-like focus when helping others. He raised awareness and money for the charity WaterAid by wearing a toilet seat during his travels. He explained that one of the things that we all must deal with when travelling is going to the toilet. Children die every year from diarrhoea and yet it's curable with a simple electrolyte solution. The right to clean water and proper sanitation is a basic human right.

Similarly, his desire to raise awareness of the perils of global warming became very real when Graham went to Tuvalu. It comprises nine islands and faces extinction because of rising seas and lashing storms. Its survival is threatened and it would be the first country that would literally be wiped off the map by climate change.

GRAHAM'S TRIUMPHANT RETURN & LEGACY

It took the Guinness Book of Records a year to sift through 10 000 photographs and over 300 hours of footage. Then, in February 2014, there was a heart-pounding moment when he saw an email notification on his phone saying 'Guinness Book of Records'. The Wi-Fi signal in the flat was awful; he was leaping around with his mobile in the air trying to get a signal. Eventually, the email opened, greeting him with the word, 'Congratulations!'

For Graham, the experience was incredible and educational. He didn't have to get into the Guinness Book of Records to validate everything he'd done. But, when they did, it made a big difference.

He became a sought-after TEDx speaker. The first was in Palm Springs and was done via a video link to Liverpool.

He wrote a travel memoir. The first was entitled 'Man of the World'. In the second book, 'Top of the World', he crosses the Himalayas. There's a third book too, 'All of the World', completing the trilogy. This links with his YouTube series of podcasts that he started in 2020, 'Hughes of the World'. These are video essays of every country in alphabetical order. It starts with a brief history of the place. Then the viewer types in a country and there is twenty-minute footage of Graham travelling in that country. He collected money from every country; cleaned it in an alcohol solution and placed them on a desk under a glass cover. There is a South African rand note (with Nelson Mandela's face); he was in the country the day it first came out.

Graham's brand will always be that of the man who proved that it was possible to travel to 201 countries with no flights. His voyage is living proof that you can still have a good time travelling this way. His quest sets him at the forefront, as the filmmaker and presenter who invited us for the ride and the vicarious thrill of his brand experience.

Initially, his branding was about his travels. Now, as the climate change agenda reverberates globally and gains momentum, his brand story is about having fun without flying. He speaks to young people in schools and universities about climate change and his brand resonates with authenticity. As CEO of NoFly Ninja, his company's first order of business was to address the serious knowledge gap that he spotted. He explained that if you use a search engine to type in Toronto to Timbuktu, it will tell you how to fly there or how to get to Mali at the very least. He is developing a website where you type in country X to country Y, anywhere in the world, and it tells you how to do the journey without flying. From his experience, he can advise travellers on how to get on cargo ships, yachts and cruise ships for part of a trip or just one leg of the cruise. He found that there are websites where they look for crew. However, it is nowhere near as effective as just going to the marina, visiting a bar and chatting to people. Nothing beats the personal touch. When he asked to be on someone's boat it was like asking people if you could stay in their house. Nobody wants to be out at sea where there was no way to escape from someone who is awful. They want to meet in person and have a chat. When the camaraderie is built, then someone would say: 'You know Bob and Lisa are going to Dominica, would you like to chat to them?' and the offer to travel with them ensues.

Six months after he finished his quest, he compiled videos with one second of his travel in every country. It went viral. When this happens, the quality of the adverts, together with your video, goes up. One Samsung advert called for applications for a game show. They advertised smartphones which had a camera with a zoom lens. He thought that would prove very useful for his travels. He filled in the application form and when asked why he should be chosen as a contestant on SOS island, Graham, who was short on time, and (as he says) with a touch of youthful arrogance wrote: 'Google me'.

The next day he received a phone call from the production company. A month later he was in Puerto Rico on a tropical island with other contestants from around the world. The experience was a lot of fun and he made life-long friends. Over six weeks, the public voted for their winner - none other than Graham. The prize was a tropical island in Panama. He lived there for the next two years with solar power; shops and civilisation a twenty-minute boat trip away, and a diet of mainly coconuts. He only bought items that could be recycled, fed to the chickens or composted.

It was a learning process. His travels taught him more than he had learnt at university. Although he was always inclined to protect the environment, he had taken electricity and running water for granted. He brought people over to the island so that they could learn how to live in a sustainable way, and he's hoping to secure funding to turn the island into an eco-retreat. In 2016, his dad was diagnosed with dementia so returned home.

But the island drew him back and, in January 2017, he returned. This was the Brexit era; Graham wrote to his local MP in Liverpool throwing down the gauntlet that if he voted with the government to scrap Article 50 without amendments and safeguards for EU citizens, he would stand against him in the next election. When Theresa May called a snap election, he returned home. He lost; it was one of the safest seats in the country. However, his brand was cemented - as the man who does what he sets out to do - whether it's going around the world without flying, winning an island or running for parliament.

He's redefining what success looks like. Graham is now forty. The nine-year-old boy who set out his quest and went on to highlight the interconnectedness between people across the globe, is living proof that the world is far kinder than we give it credit for. His brand story tells us that we can travel through life on our own terms. But we should never forget to be compassionate to our planet and grateful to those who help us on this journey. His brand also examines the blunt instruments we use to define success.

When he was doing talks around the country, he contacted an old school friend. They got together. Now, he no longer chats up bikini-clad women; he's too busy being a suburban stepdad to two girls.

Values underpinning story branding:

- Protect the environment by not flying.

- Alleviate poverty.

- Reduce carbon footprint.

- Raise awareness and money for charity WaterAid.

- Demonstrate that the world isn't such a terrifying place.

When he was about 21, he worked to save up for a trip to India. He told a friend that he was going alone. The friend looked at him and said: 'You will die.'

At that point, he had only travelled to the Middle East. He told me: 'I had seen enough of the world by then to know it's not as bad as a lot of people think. So, one of the main drivers behind this, aside from the environmental thinking, was to show that the world wasn't such a terrifying place because of the sensationalist news stories that give us a distorted view.'

While travelling, he never fell ill, was never mugged and was never robbed. No matter how poor people were, they welcomed him, shared their food, and went out of their way to help him. This Brit with grit says: 'I found very quickly that you just keep smiling no matter how tired or pissed off you are. No matter how long you've been on the train or the bus, just keep smiling.'

We ended our interview and Graham said that he was going to make a bunny chow for his stepdaughters, and they were going to talk about it.

Global Scouse Day

Graham and his then-girlfriend invited friends over to their flat for his birthday.

They would have Scouse which is like Irish stew - onions, carrots, potatoes and meat. You put it on the hob and leave it to cook for hours and hours. This slow cooking captures all the flavours and results in a very tasty, winter-warming dish.

It has its humble origins with sailors from Norway. After spending six months at sea, eating ship's biscuits, their boats would dock in the mornings and they would go to the pub for food. The stew would be heated, and they would enjoy a hot, hearty meal.

At the end of 2008, he set off on his journey around the world to every country. He had a friend in Liverpool who started to do a Scouse meal on his birthday. In his absence, she persuaded restaurants and bars around

Liverpool to put Scouse on the menu. It took off. Today there are over 100 bars and restaurants, including some high-end eateries, that put Scouse on their menus.

There is a video of former Liverpool FC John Aldridge cooking up the perfect Scouse, and more recently Everton serving up this now-famous dish on Global Scouse Day. Every year, since 2012, Scouse has been distributed to a homeless charity in Liverpool.

His legacy and branding as a hero locally and globally are such that even in his absence it grew organically. Graham believes that it is a way to get everyone involved. He is trying to set up a meeting between Liverpool and Manchester to create the carbon natural challenge. It is intended to be a fight between Liverpool and Manchester to see which can be carbon neutral first. The rivalry between the two cities is well known and he likens it to a Hollywood movie where humans get together to fight the common enemy. In this case, to become carbon neutral to secure the future of our children.

WHAT IS A BRAND?

According to Baines, Fill & Rosengren[2], branding is a process by which sellers help customers differentiate between offerings. An offering is a product, service or experience.

- Graham's offerings have a unique selling point (USP). He was invited by TEDx to deliver talks on this unique experience - no one else has first-hand knowledge of going around the world without flying.

- He lived on an island without electricity and water so when he talks at schools and universities about how to reduce the effects of climate change, he speaks from a position of authenticity.

- He appeared on CNN, National Geographic, major newspapers and magazines globally because his brand inspires countries and individuals.

- His products - films, vlogs, talks, website, book and articles reflect the values inherent in his quest.

- He provided an experience on his island, where he demonstrated his brand in action.

WHY DO WE BRAND? [3]

- Customers use brands to help them identify the offerings they prefer to satisfy their needs and wants. Let's say you are celebrating your birthday this weekend. Your partner decides that you will go out for your meal and books a table at your favourite restaurant to meet your need to eat in a place whose brand you trust. Friends and family buy gifts from brands that you like, to satisfy your wants. *More of this in Chapter 6.*

- Brands are offerings from a known source that add value. Brands evoke feelings in the consumer about the brand's attributes and performance. The consumer is the person who uses the offering and the customer is the buyer. So, if your partner bought you this book, she is the customer, but you are reading it, so that makes you the consumer.

- Although marketing teams create and sustain a brand, it is the marketing team and the customer that co-create the brand. *More of this in Chapters 4 and 7.*

How do you Build a Brand?

Building a brand is like building a house:

- You are the project manager or storyteller. As such, you have a grip on every facet of the building - planning your story, your niche, the tone of language used to engage your customers, risks, strengths, timeline, costing, and the marketing platforms for unveiling your story.

- First, you choose a plot.

- If you've inherited the plot, you must decide whether to keep the original building or demolish part of it. This step is crucial as companies try to stay afloat during the pandemic impact and aftershocks.

- The architect's drawing is the vision - From planning to implementation and follow-up.

- Your foundation is the bedrock of the building. This is what influences your customers. How do they feel when they enter your house? Is your house safe? Value for money? Or a high-end brand?

- The building bricks are the elements of your story. Does it elicit empathy? How did you feel when Graham was thrown in a filthy prison cell, stripped and deprived of outside contact?

- Your personal and company values are the cement that holds the house together and pervades the building. Even if a part of the structure breaks, your foundation or root is resilient. You change the materials to progress.

- The decorating - Tiles, paint colour, awnings, blinds are used to get visitors to the door. If you are doing online marketing, it means clicks and heeding the call to action.

- The quality of the materials is similar to the way you craft your story. It can make your brand or damage it.

THE PSYCHOLOGY OF STORY BRANDING

Social psychologists[4] tell us that from ancient times leaders and marketers relied on stories to change people's attitudes, beliefs and behaviour. They found that stories have the power to persuade and change the reader's attitude. The latter is mentally transported into the world depicted in the story and returns from this journey with a change in attitude. Their research reiterated that the story message can persuade the reader to make a huge shift in attitude. This change is greater when stories are written with compelling arguments and have a clear, strong plot.

There are two important implications as you build the foundation to your story:

- You need a clear, strong plotline.

- Your marketing message should be embedded in your story.

LET'S LOOK AT GRAHAM'S PLOT

WHAT'S HIS STORY?

The plot is a voyage and return story. In terms of his determination to be the first person to visit every country without flying, it has the element of a quest.

According to Booker, with a quest, there is a 'priceless goal, worth any effort to achieve: a treasure; a promised land, something of infinite value.'[5] When the hero hears of this treasure, he will set out on a dangerous journey to attain it and it becomes the most important thing to him. No matter the peril, he will not rest until he returns home victorious.

Booker outlines the stages of the voyage and return:[6]

Anticipation: The hero is curious and looks for something to happen. He then ventures into a world that he never experienced before.

Initial Fascination or Dream Stage: At first this adventure is exhilarating.

Frustration Stage: Then frustration, difficulties and oppression take place.

Nightmare Stage: These frustrations grow until they threaten the hero's survival.

Thrilling Escape and Return Stage: Just as it becomes too much to bear, the hero prevails, returns and explores how the voyage has changed him and what he has learnt from it.

Consider

- Is your plot a voyage and return?

- Does it have a quest element?

- What is your company's unique selling point (USP)? What have you done or created that no one else has?

- What do you want your legacy to be?

- What rules or slogan did you form as you made your journey to your present point? How can you use these for your brand story?

- During lockdown and with the pandemic fallout, how will you establish camaraderie without face-to-face rapport-building?

COACHING QUESTIONS FOR MY

BRAND STORY

- How do I tell my story to reflect my company's vision?

- What do I use to build my foundation to influence my customers and future customers?

- When have I used my story bricks to elicit my customers' empathy or retain them? How do I know this?

- How do I convey our personal and company values to persuade customers?

- During an unprecedented global crisis like COVID-19, how do we pivot and remain true to our value system?

- What materials do I use to reflect the nature and benefits of our offerings and couch it in language that is simple but has evocative literary elements?

- Who do I need to speak to about getting the perfect blend of business and literary language without compromising any of the above?

- What instruments will I use to measure the extent to which my story has persuaded customers?

To summarise, building a brand is like the construction of a house. You need a strong plot and building blocks that reflect your vision and values, and a clear way to make your offering stand out. In the next chapter we look at a master on a quest for gold and how to embed branding elements to cement your story.

Chapter Two

The Master's quest

When Donald Brown was ten, he fell in love. Like all first loves it consumed him. And continued to do so for years. It wasn't until four years later that he plucked up the courage to bring his passion to his home: a lump of squishy clay that he intended to use to sculpt his head. As he began working at the kitchen table his mum and dad said: 'Good night, Donald.'

The house was silent until he heard his parents say: 'Good morning, Donald.'

We know that the course of true love never did run smooth. After introducing his love for sculpture to his family, his quest to fulfil this passion was defined by a question from his mum: 'What is this playing with mud going to do for you?'

Like any son who brings home a girl mum doesn't approve of, he knew that she loved him dearly, but it didn't lessen the pain of rejection for his cherished art.

His parents were Jamaican and, like most West Indian families in 1960s England, life was a struggle. The never-ending hand-me-downs from his older brother was a constant reminder of this. The young boy who dreamt of being a figurative sculptor knew that this was not the done-thing. He didn't have a Michelangelo, Rodin or Bernini with whom he could identify with, or learn from. His passion was equally unacceptable to his community. They believed that you had to be well-connected, gifted and lucky to evade the starving artist stereotype. First love or not, many thought he had none of these qualities. Add to this a serious case of asthma and you had, well - not much to work with.

That's what many thought. Not Donald. He decided that his environment may be hostile towards his art, but he had the resources that could alter his destiny. You see, that night, Donald didn't just produce a sculpture of his head. He branded his life by building the vision that would defy all the odds stacked against him. While he knew that his mum was well-intentioned, her response was the catalyst for him to learn and practise the art of turning negative into positive. He decided to ignore the discouragement, disapproval or lack of enthusiasm from those around him. He was crystal clear on one thing - he was going to nurture his art. Slowly but consistently. At fourteen, he appeared on national TV in a children's art exhibition. Then, just as Donald was mapping out this path, he became smitten with another love, sport.

The Call

He completed secondary school and, to please his mum, agreed to become a minister. He visited a seminary college and asked for the art department. He was told that there wasn't one. He ditched that decision and made one of his own. He spent a gap year as an art technician and then did a degree in Fine Art Sculpture. How was he going to rise above his setbacks? He decided that he wasn't going to wait for doors to open because he already held the keys to the right doors. His slogan was moulded: 'Look not to others to grant you that which you already have.'

THE JOURNEY

In 1997, he sold his cherished status symbol car to raise money. Donald decided to pursue his art in America. He went to an arts festival and ended up staying there for ten years. His so-called friends told him that he would amount to nothing. With both his art and sport he would be the jack of all trades and master of none. Their derision rang in his ears: 'Who does he think he is, holding his head up high?'

It was a supreme irony that he was told he would master nothing. Within a month of being in America, his sculptures were noticed. He was featured on radio, TV, magazines and newspapers. At one point, he was broadcast on satellite TV into 100 million homes in 177 countries. His quest led to him meeting celebrities like Beyoncé, Babyface, Whitney Houston and Colin Powell. Word got back to the naysayers; they saw photos of Donald with his sculptures, meeting celebrities, and the same friends said: 'That's our Donald. We always knew he would make it.'

Whilst in America, he heard about the USA Heptathlon Championships. He had not trained in athletics for a while but had played volleyball at home and was in good shape. He entered and won gold to become the National USA Champion. A few weeks later he entered the National Pentathlon and won gold. Donald was 42 and decided to give his athletics career another run. When he returned to the UK, he entered the National Decathlon Championships and, yes, there's a theme emerging; he won gold.

THE FINAL ORDEAL

Donald began to feel like all the sacrifices he had made to undertake the journey to America had been worth it. Then, one day, he received news from home. His parents had become frail; they needed care. He travelled back to the UK immediately and put his quest on hold. It was time-consuming work being a carer, but he accepted it as a blessing. His dad passed away and his mum was diagnosed with dementia. Her care was beyond his scope of expertise and so sought professional help for her.

COMPANIONS

He returned to court his two equal passions, both of which were time-consuming and demanding. Donald trained for ten events and found it exhausting. His friend, Masters athlete Dalton Powell, advised him that the times in which he was running the 100m was comparable to the pure sprinters in his age group. He competed in the 2009 European Masters Indoor Championship and came second in the indoor 60m sprint, pipped to the post in two 100ths of a second by none other than Dalton. Donald took it as a steer in his athletics journey, bid farewell to the decathlon, and began to focus on sprints, long jumps and hurdles.

Donald's coach from his early 20s was former GB International and Masters World Champion, Joseph Caines. When Donald moved to London his new companions were a group of Masters athletes anchored by former professional footballer and Masters athlete, Leon Braithwaite and his brother, Darren Braithwaite. Darren competed with icons of track and field like Carl

Lewis and Linford Christie. Donald attributes his success to the fun-loving rivalry of the squad and the coaches he was privileged to work with.

He began his Masters Athletics journey and, in true Donald style, had his eye on gold.

He acknowledges that we aren't going to be as fast as we were twenty or thirty years ago. However, it was about showing that, after 35, you can still have the mindset and a physicality that is healthy. He said: 'I like competition as a target. Some people can go to the gym and train and train and I admire them. I have no desire to get in great shape and do nothing with it. For me, it's about training to compete with the best in the world.'

He looked within himself. While he believed that he had done ok in the last few years, he felt that he could do better. He decided that he was not going to train as hard as when he was a kid. It was about quality, not quantity. He diagnosed his physical weakness and designed some unique exercises that strengthened those areas.

He used a sledge, added weights to it and walked with it. Athletes at the Stadium laughed at him when they saw this. However, the sledge walking allowed him to slow down the whole process of running to a walking motion and to focus on every area of strength. He got a real intense lactic and glutes burn from this slow session rather than ten sessions. He couldn't walk the next day but had a great feeling of rejuvenation. He shared his ideas with others.

In athletics, where wins and losses are counted in microseconds, and sportsmen and women are becoming faster, fitter and climbing higher, what made him stand out from the crowd?

Donald followed his heart. He realised that sometimes you just have to shut out all the noise, analyse what you are doing, and believe in yourself. He became an award-winning sculptor. He wanted to help young people follow their dreams and is now a motivational speaker, who uses art and sport as the drivers to promote peace. He founded his company the Global Gallery with the mission 'Inspiring present and future generations'. He started talking about his sculptures and its symbolism. He visits schools, centres and youth clubs. As they answer his questions, he puts his medals around their necks to give them a feel for victory. He wants to make a difference in their lives. He realised that those who told him he couldn't do more than one thing, or wouldn't make it in America, or that he would amount to nothing, were trying to limit him because they felt like they couldn't chase their dreams. His vision was simple because he was living it:

- Take charge of your dreams and never let others derail you.

- Set your goals and control your mental journey.

- Self-awareness leads to good choices, while fear and insecurities tinge decisions that are made for you.

- Grow and learn from your failures.

- Give back to others.

Donald's embarrassment of riches continued. He's been steadily bringing home the bling for his country, culminating in winning three gold medals at the European Championships, becoming World Champion in the 60m hurdles and ranking No.1 in the world for four events in 2019. In 2020, at 56 years of age, he broke the British record for the 60m hurdles; a few weeks later, in the UK National Masters Championships in London, he broke the British record in the 60m sprint. In February 2020, he gained the coveted award for being the male runner up for the World Masters Athletics Award 2019 in the sprints category.

His Legacy

Donald's vision to follow his true north led to an ambitious global peace initiative. As an award-winning sculptor, Masters World Champion and inspirational speaker, he uses his sculptures as visual aids to discuss positive life principles like humility, healing, forgiveness and peace. His work reflects his advocacy for addressing gang culture and working against bullying.

He believes that no matter what material you start off with, in this instance a 'muddy mess', you can still build a masterpiece. When we experience inner peace on our journey, we give personal peace a chance. He uses his sculpture 'A Sporting Chance for Peace' and identifies cities around the world that have proven to reduce crime, knife crime, bullying and violence and presents them with a replica of the sculpture. This will continue for ten years with his tagline 'A Decade of Peace'.

This is a great responsibility for one sculpture. However, it is no ordinary sculpture. It took four years to produce the masterpiece. It depicts sportsmen and women whose stances are richly embedded in the symbolism of values and life skills that encapsulate success, good choices and the responsibility to contribute to peace.

A hurdler is at the centre of the sculpture. We can't help wondering if life was imitating art, as a few years after the sculpture was completed, Donald won gold at the World Masters Championship for 60m hurdles. He poses the question to his young audience: 'Are you choosing the right hurdles?'

He refers to gang violence and knife crime. Before gaining membership in a gang, there is a hurdle for the initiate. Does this person choose to jump this hurdle? Or do you make the choice to choose other hurdles like passing exams and entering higher education? Are we taking on the right challenges that lead to success or the ones that steer us in the wrong direction? Sometimes, youngsters choose the wrong challenges because they want to feel included and accepted. When you lose your identity, you end up standing for nothing that really matters. He cited the example of how capricious the fashion industry is. One summer, influencers tell you that short skirts are in and masses follow. He shows young people that they should not lose the ability to think for themselves; to analyse and process.

The extended metaphor of the rowing team stays faithful to Donald's early decisions to be true to oneself. Sometimes we do as we are told by our family and friends because we respect them and wish to please them. This can be a precursor for a crisis. When you get to a certain point in life, you feel trapped in the life that was custom-made by others. We surround ourselves with the wrong company; people that steer us in the direction that isn't right for us. This may lead to a life of crime, drugs and gangs.

We move on to the woman athlete passing on the baton to the outgoing male athlete who depicts the need to pass it to the next generation. If we fail to do this, then we can't enable them. He receives feedback from his audiences who tell him that they pursued their passion because of what they heard from him and said that he realised that he didn't have to stand in a church to make a difference in others' lives.

We are led to cyclists who demonstrate the cycle of life. The back wheel of the cyclist is a wheelchair which represents the disadvantages that we all have to varying degrees. Adjacent to this, the diver takes the plunge and shows that despite our challenges we must forge ahead. Beside the diver is the tennis player, whose back and forth actions illustrate indecisiveness. The skater on thin ice reassures the viewer that it's ok to fail.

When Donald speaks to young people about A Sporting Chance for Peace, he points out the shadows that we all fall prey to. He refers to the surfer riding a wave. However, the wave emerges from the shadows. These shadows define us through the minds and eyes of others and preclude us from shaping our destinies. We live in the shadow of others because we don't strike out on our own and live a life filled with regret and missed opportunities.

The Goal

His vision is to work towards an academy where students train under him to realise that the message within their work is as important as creativity itself. There are brilliant artists whose works are very violent, profane and sexually oriented. He wishes to leave a legacy where his art humanises and resonates with the masses. Art shouldn't be about chasing money. Once you have something of substance, the demand ensues.

Years ago, during his American stay, Donald visited a North Carolina church and began talking to the bishop. The latter stopped him and asked him to deliver two sermons on Sunday to a congregation of about 3,000. He also asked him to bring any sculpture prints that he had to hand. That Sunday, he sold many prints, wrote a 4-figure cheque and gifted it to the church. He realised that when you have something of substance and a message that people can connect to, they will want you and your offering.

When he appeared on international TV, the congregation from their local church told his mum (who never watches TV) that he was ministering through his art.

One day he was working on A Sporting Chance for Peace and brought it home. He related a conversation he had with his mum as she looked at the sculpture.

Donald (imitating his mum's Jamaican accent): Donald, but who made the faces?

Donald: I did.

Mum: The eyes, you did that? You are good.

Weeks later she asked: The face is so good. You did that?

After four decades, his first love was welcomed home and received his mum's blessing.

How Your Brand Helps Customers

According to Baines et al[1], brands save customers time and risk in avoiding brands that they dislike. These risks can be:

- **Financial**: Can I afford this car?

- **Social:** What will other people think about me if I wear this dress on a date?

- **Functional**: Will these blinds blackout the morning sun?

Crucially, branding helps consumers develop relationships based on trust and respect. They add that by crafting a strong brand story your company can:

- **Develop customer trust, loyalty and repeat purchases**: Let's say you're doing your grocery shopping and are looking for cereal. You skim the shelves and grab the brand you've been eating for years.

- **Increase the value of the company**: The stronger your narrative, the greater the influence on your customer and the greater the profits.

- **Enable higher pricing**: While shopping, you avoid the no-name brands and look for your favourite brand. It is priced higher because it elicits the feel-good factor that it is superior.

- **Deter competitors from entering your niche**: In recent years, the vegan market has exploded with plant-based protein and fake meat. Although Nestlé[2] entered only recently, their branding as an established food manufacturer will deter smaller companies from entering the vegan market.

- **Gives you a competitive advantage**: Car makers, Tesla, had a goal[3] of building cars with power and sleek looks with zero emissions. After the success of their Model S, where they received top scores from industry experts, they were recognised as a leading brand in electric plug-in cars.

- **Gives legal protection**: In 2009, Gucci sued Guess[4] claiming that Guess had copied their logo for a line of shoes. They filed two claims in New York and Milan. They won an award of $4.7 million in damages in New York but lost in Milan as they were told that the symbol G is common in the fashion industry.

When Donald puts his medals around the necks of his young audience, he is creating a relationship with them that is based on trust and loyalty. The next time the customer (headteacher) wants a speaker for her consumers (students), she's going to think about how Donald made her students feel. Based on this, she would be inclined to make a repeat purchase of his services. Donald's story branding gives him a competitive advantage. When the medal is placed on a wide-eyed youngster, for that brief moment in time that youngster is Donald himself, the Masters champion, who has just won gold. This story brand, underpinned by trust and respect, deters competitors from entering that particular school.

Taglines, Slogans, Vision Statements and Mission

According to Prater[5], taglines are like verbal logos and act as triggers. Taglines say who you are and what you represent: Tottenham Hotspur's[6] tagline is: 'Audere est Facere' or 'To Dare is to Do'.

Slogans sum up a company strategy and tell you why you should choose their product or service: Audi's slogan[7] is 'Vorsprung durch Technik' meaning 'Advancement through Technology'.

A company's mission statement outlines the objectives and goals in a succinct statement: The Global Gallery is 'A Decade of Peace'.

A vision statement outlines your long-term goals and how it will inspire staff to achieve it.

What's His Story?

The hero goes on a quest. As we learnt in chapter one, from the moment the hero becomes aware of the goal, he sets off on a dangerous journey to secure the prize. Donald's quest is two-fold. The first is to pursue his love for sculpture and become a globally recognised artist. The second is his athletics journey where he quite literally goes for gold. Implicit in these quests is Donald's desire to be true to himself; to follow his dreams and take others on his journey. He gains gold in his athletics journey and becomes a sculptor who produces masterpieces that gain popularity with both ordinary folk and A-listers. He is consistently driven by the need to mould present and future generations; to minister and serve.

Booker[8] shows that the quest story has stages:

- **The Call**: The hero realises that his life is oppressive, and he needs to make a journey to set things right. Donald makes his journey to university even though he has none of the advantages that will bring success in his chosen field and is discouraged from doing so by those around him.

- **The Journey**: The hero and his companions set off on this quest. Donald left for America and on his return to the UK he moved to London.

- **Frustration**: He was derided by those who had no faith in his quest.

- **The Final Ordeal**: The hero must pass a series of tests.

- **The Goal**: The treasure and the promise of renewed life are attained. Donald won gold, silver and bronze medals, broke athletics records, and became a world-acclaimed sculptor. His story encompassing his art and sport secured his legacy.

Consider:

- Is yours a quest story?

- How do you use story branding in an intense burn to build relationships with consumers rather than a series of rapid-fire marketing?

- What enabled Donald to sell his prints to complete strangers at that church in North Carolina? What can you take from this to add to your brand story?

Coaching Questions for

My Brand story

- What aids can I use to enhance my story message? Donald uses his award-winning sculptures as props, backdrop and characters to brand.

- How does our slogan serve to persuade customers?

- How does the tone of the tagline contribute to my brand?

- In what way does our mission statement contribute to our brand?

- How do I tell my story to evoke empathy?

- What do I want our legacy to be? How will I convey this in my story?

- How can we niche our offering to make our brand story stand out?

- What can I do so that our offering makes our consumers feel the way those youngsters did?

- How do I tell my story to get repeat purchases?

To sum up, we looked at how brands help customers and why we need to brand.

In the next chapter you will solidify your brand story foundation, make a promise to your consumers, and differentiate between successful and failing brands.

Chapter Three

Badass Dream Builder

Arya Taware's dad was the black sheep of the family. He was the youngest of seven children and at sixteen, he decided that he wasn't going to follow in the tradition of sugarcane farming. He took the unprecedented step of leaving home to enrol for a college diploma in Pune. He was the first person in his family to cross the boundaries of his tiny village. He was raised in grinding poverty, unable even to afford shoes. The bus ticket for the entire journey to college was out of his reach. He solved this by making part of the journey by bus and then cycling the remainder of the way. He fed himself with the food he carried from home. And the will to succeed.

He married young. Arya's mum painted pictures with her hand on the walls of their home, the size of a tiny London office cubicle. Her dad secured a job in government and while it was a junior position, it was considered very prestigious. After working there for six years, he decided that he wanted more from life. He started investing in property. Arya was born; an Indian girl in a country entrenched in centuries of patriarchy. When families would attend a function, the tradition was that the men would go off to one corner of the room and discuss politics and business, while the women and girls would gather in another corner and talk about household matters. Not Arya, she was having none of it. She would follow her dad to be with the men and boys, and her dad in turn, treated her like a son. Like him, she was an avid reader and she nurtured her risk-taking by learning about entrepreneurs like Richard Branson and Kiran Mazumdar-Shaw who overcame setbacks to achieve huge success.

Arya continued to defy boundaries and forge an entrepreneurial way of doing things. When she was eighteen, she set her sights on London and left India to do her primary degree in Urban Planning at University College London. After living in luxury from her teenage years, she started her journey from practically nothing. She was alone, in a foreign city, and without any resources. She was undaunted as she had watched her dad rise in the property market in such a short space of time without any backing. She rolled up her sleeves.

Building the Foundation

After graduating, she worked for a small house builder in London. Her job description was to look for potential sites for development, make sure the numbers stacked up and ensure that planning was in place. This was an eye-opener as she saw first-hand what small to medium enterprise (SME) housebuilders were confronted with when they attempted to secure funding. She started obsessing over this problem. She wanted to learn more about why this was happening, so she read all the government reports and realised that it was SMEs' inability to access mainstream finance that was holding them back. The government stopped building homes as banking regulations became stricter and tighter. The SMEs were the first to bear the brunt of this. Later, she worked in the planning department at a Local Authority where she learnt how the council's bigger sites were sold to house builders and how planning permission was granted.

Arya booked her place in laying the foundation for the construction industry when she spotted this gap in the market for SME house builders. She was going to help them build their dreams. Armed with this experience and foresight she cast her sights on the burgeoning peer-to-peer (P2P) lending scene in New York and met founders of other real estate P2P lending platforms at a time when it was still a niche concept in the UK. She founded her company, FutureBricks with the brand promise: 'Breaking the brick ceiling.'

It proved to be both operational and prophetic. Arya wanted to give back after being inspired by other entrepreneurs' journeys she had read about. FutureBricks logo was done in graffiti style; inspired by the artist Banksy. It connotes a badass and gives the explicit message that FutureBricks is there for the common people, which contrasts with most financial institutions that are stodgy traditional lenders.

Similarly, the property sector is steeped in age-old tradition and is dominated by men. Arya faced many challenges regarding her age and gender. She was one of the youngest alternative lending leaders in the country, a woman, and an immigrant. The first image that Arya shattered was that of an alternative lender. She was constantly told that she was too young and found that, of the discrimination that she confronted, 70% was ageism. The remainder was sexism. I asked her about racism. She said that she hadn't experienced it probably because the ageism and sexism had been so direct and extreme, and by the time some investors had waded through these murky waters, they were probably too worn out to worry about that. Clearly, a lady with a game plan.

She recounted two cases of sexism that she had encountered. The first time she became angry when she was asked about her marriage plans. However, she was learning quickly; especially how to navigate the unexpected. And she was consciously branding herself and her company as one that breaks all ceilings, glass or otherwise. There was an exchange of texts between a potential wealthy, 'sophisticated' investor and a go-between who was helping her raise capital:

Investor's forwarded text: 'The business plan is good. Everything is great. I like the idea, but I have one question. Previously I invested in a female-led business and she had to move away because of her family. So, she closed the business down. What are Arya's plans? Is she with someone? Is her personal life stable?

Arya's reply text to go-between: 'I had also invested in one business. It was a great business plan and a male-led business. All the money that was raised went to massive salaries rather than investing in the business. Eventually, the business was shut down. So, what was his plan?'

Arya's youth and gender still elicit surprise and sometimes shock when she walks into a room. However, as soon as she starts talking, she gains instant respect because this entrepreneur knows what she's talking about. She believes that she learnt how to be an adult as she was building her business. Usually, people grow up first and then grow a business but her maturity and startup intertwined. She had to figure out everything after leaving university. There wasn't any financial support, so she learnt how to do everything - pay for food, rent and build the business, which, at the beginning wasn't going anywhere. 'It was very challenging, but it made me very strong as a person. It tested every bone in my body. If you really want to be an entrepreneur, and I'm so glad this is true, what doesn't kill you will make you stronger. When you don't have a plan B or backup option you just have to move forward. That's how I saw it. This was it. I have to follow my dreams.'

The biggest hurdle was getting finance, and the company needed capital from the get-go. With the backing of twenty angel investors, Arya managed to raise £1 million in equity and launched FutureBricks in 2018. She started her business from scratch, was regulated by the Financial Conduct Authority (FCA), built the technology, handpicked her core team, and a strong board of industry experts. It took almost two years to build this. In one year, FutureBricks funded seven projects and achieved a loan book of £1 million. There are now 1,000 lenders on their platform. They proved that they could source the deal, underwrite it and fund it. 2020 is all about growth and fun stuff. In one year, they did proof of concept.

WHAT MAKES HER STORY BRAND

SO COMPELLING?

She decided early on that she wanted to be an entrepreneur and to be independent. No matter the scale of the setbacks, giving up was never an option for her and it never once crossed her mind to think what she could do if her startup didn't work out. There were tears, distress and dark days. She woke up the next morning and started again. She believed in her idea. And in herself.

Arya shaped her personal brand and company brand at the same time. She was a university graduate and had never been employed before. She did it in stages. She met with 200-300 people initially for investment. Once she landed the first big investment, she started building the prototype. There was traction and proof. She is quick to reassure that irrespective of your age, being an entrepreneur is a struggle, like a walk in the dark. Success is about probability. If you reach out to 100 people, only one will convert. If you reach out to 500, probably 25 will convert. It's about doing more to get what you want and growing a thick skin by not taking comments to heart.

BUILDING A STORY BRAND

After raising equity in the early stages of the business, a second challenge was meeting the right shareholders or partners. In the initial stages, Arya, like most entrepreneurs, was short on negotiation power and made the typical entrepreneur's mistake of not shaking hands with the right people. However, part of her growth is learning to clean up and learn from them. Now, she's at the stage where she can smell a bad deal. She attributes her mistakes to her age and gender. When she was 22 (she's now 26) she was naive, and as a woman, more trusting. She has developed her brand to such an extent that she can let go of a deal that doesn't come through, knowing that a better one will emerge. It's the same with her investors. This attitude reflects the ethics that mark FutureBricks which were in place from day one and are never compromised. There are three non-negotiables:

- Customer honesty - They will walk away from a deal or an investor who doesn't reflect this.

- Sterling service.

- The quality of the loan book and the underwriting process.

It's not just about fulfilling her dream of helping build dreams for those in the SME market. It is also about preserving the planet. When they are in a stronger position to command it, they will ask for statistics relating to sustainability. They are lenders and the ones who are giving the money so they can command the numbers on some of the following:

- What is the EPC (property's energy efficiency) rating following a build?

- How much onsite waste can be recycled?

- How many trees were there?

- How many were removed?

- Have you planted the same amount or double the amount?

Arya and her generation will bear the brunt of the effects of climate change and she believes that if she doesn't do something about this on a personal or business level, she will be failing her generation. She points out that they are thinking ahead but are not there yet.

MARKETING STRATEGY

Since its inception, marketing wasn't a priority as they didn't have the budget for it. So how did they draw their lenders?

A previous shareholder's company sponsored events that enabled them to infiltrate communities. It was relatively cheap and enabled them to access 200 people by using some stage time to present. It wasn't a scalable strategy but a good start. As they did more events, they learnt which events were good and negotiated with the organisers for more stage time. Some were private sessions. Then they realised that most of their customers were doctors and tapped into the communities that were doing annual sponsorships. This entailed many physical and manual processes. Their product is so good that they were able to get investors. In addition, the barrier to enter was only £500, so people were willing to bet on it. For some lenders, anything between £10K and £20K was not a big amount.

On the borrowing side, it was a lot simpler. They found a planning database and reached out in a very cost-effective way. It's actually zero cost for outsourcing the borrowing site because they are a market-based platform. It is much harder for them as most of the businesses have just one platform but for them, there are two separate processes, as they have customers from the lenders and borrowers' sides. It's like the marketplace of uber drivers and riders' marketplace platforms. In 2021, they envisage a marketing budget and will get onto social media.

Arya's grit and the way in which she met with challenges shows that she really is a badass player. What story marketing advice does she have for other entrepreneurs?

She is valued for her honesty as that equates to integrity. Part of this honesty is about her struggle. It contributes to the creation of the work culture and is reflective of her integrity which is modelled in a top-down approach for the company. She's numbers-driven and a very logical person, which is a precursor for sticking to the point and saying it like it is.

Arya is a gamechanger in the construction and FinTech industries and when I asked her what advice she would give to girls wanting to break into these fields, she replied with her trademark brutal honesty. She confessed that she hated maths at school and was slightly dyslexic. If a number is said very fast, she will have to ask you to repeat it three times. The irony that she heads a finance business is not lost on her. However, her company lends money and she has a full underwriting team who are highly skilled with numbers, analysis and stress testing. And therein lies the rub. What this entrepreneurial leader knows is that she needs operational knowledge, is passionate about her niche business and knows how to recruit talented employees. She clarified with an example. If she was asked to do a development appraisal, she would be clueless as she doesn't know the step-by-step formula. However, she could look at an appraisal and assess whether it was sound as she knows the principles underlying it. She observed that women are very safe by nature. In contrast, a man even if he doesn't know much will say: 'Yeah, I can do this'. Then he will go off and figure it out or get help and present it with confidence. We can't know everything in life.

Arya was featured in newspapers, magazines, TV and radio and picked up many accolades. Some of these include the Business Insider's Top 40 Coolest People in FinTech and City A.M's 25 under 25. When I asked her how she had impacted FinTech and construction as a Millennial woman she said: 'I still feel I have a long way to go on my journey. I want to be successful in a way that breaks even consistently. Until I reach that, I don't feel that I should be a role model because for me it's about proving and showing that my success is sustainable. I'm hoping that it happens in 2020.'

I asked her to define what success would look like. Her reply: She would feel like she has put a dent in the market in 3.5 years when FutureBricks was a 100 million loan bank.

I know, I had to read that three times as well.

The Strength of FutureBricks

Brand Story

According to Chernatony and Riley[1], the difference between successful and failed brands is whether the values the company develops for the brand matches the consumers' emotional and rational needs.

The rational need for FutureBricks borrowers was finance to build. Their emotional needs were that the funding they received from this new P2P lender was a safe bet and that they would be treated fairly. In order to brand successfully for both borrowers and investors Arya's brand matched her borrowers' needs by:

- Identifying why SMEs were not being given loans by traditional bankers.

- Designing and packaging a niche service to fill this gap.

- Meticulous research to see how this was done successfully elsewhere.

- Securing the right team to support her.

- Getting under a regulatory umbrella.

- Marketing to find lenders and borrowers.

- Building relationships of trust with lenders and borrowers.

- Maintaining the integrity of the loan book.

- Maintaining passion and enthusiasm for the idea.

- Developing a sound product that withstood barriers.

- Unflinching belief in her idea.

- Showing entrepreneurial leadership.

- Tackling barriers like ageism and sexism head on.

- Ethics like honesty underpinning the business.

- A name, logo and promise that reflects the above practice.

- Numbers based laser-focus on sustainability and growth.

The Three Brand Ps

Brands make promises and successful brands evoke strong feelings. Baines et al[2] refer to the Three Brand Ps (3BPs), promises, positioning and performance.

Central to this 3BPs is communication which:

- Enables a promise to be made (brand awareness).

- Positions the brand correctly (brand attitude).

- Delivers brand performance (brand response).

According to Baines et al[3], brand positioning is a strategic activity where we differentiate and distinguish a brand so that the consumer understands it and remembers it. Some companies add to this relational branding, with the aim to attract relationship-oriented customers. Gardner[4] tells us that brand thinking is about relationship building and calls for authenticity and engagement.

Finkle[5] elaborates that a brand promise is a sentence or two outlining the customer's expectations. For new brands, it's about forming customer expectations.

When writing your brand promise Workfront[6] asks us to ensure that it is simple, credible, different, memorable and inspiring.

We know the legendary brands' promises:

Apple promises to 'Think different'.

Lego's Play Promise: 'Joy of Building, Pride of Creation'.

Virgin Atlantic: 'To be genuine, fun, contemporary and different in everything we do at a reasonable price'.

Mercedes: 'The best or nothing'.

Nike: 'To bring inspiration and innovation to every athlete* in the world.' *They clarify that if you have a body, you're an athlete. How inspirational and encouraging is that!

Now, you are probably wondering how you can come up with a brand promise that is as legendary as that. Let's look at FutureBrick's brand promise: 'Breaking the brick wall'. It is:

Simple: Four short words but with a deep wealth of connotation speaking to Arya's badass, youthful brand.

Credible: SMEs met with a brick wall when they tried to borrow from traditional banks. So did Arya when she arrived in London as a young, Asian female immigrant. This not only elicits empathy but deepens the relationship between her brand and the customers who are underdogs in the face of traditional banking and giant construction. Who amongst us doesn't root for the underdog?

Different: A play on Arya completely ignoring the fragile glass ceiling to stamp her company's trademark and performance on the P2P lending scene. As a FinTech woman, she's chosen something more solid to infiltrate, and dominate.

Memorable: It reminds the consumer what industry her brand deals with and the authenticity of her story makes it inspiring.

The promise not only sets her up for legendary status but imbues her followers with a vested interest in her brand success.

WHAT'S HER STORY?

Booker[7] tells us that in the rags to riches story, the heroine leaves behind obscurity and poverty to rise to a life of splendour and happiness. The stages are:

- **Initial unhappiness and the call**: The patriarchal society in which Arya was raised and the desire to be treated equally by all in society. Her fascination with London and role models like Richard Branson, was the call.

- **Out into the world, initial success**: The heroine is rewarded with initial success, but it is not without ordeal. Arya gets her degree but struggles to manage financially in London. She founded FutureBricks.

- **The central crisis**: The challenge of how to raise capital as a young, untested girl in the FinTech and construction industry in a foreign country. She's not invited to the party as it's men only. So, she gate-crashes the biggest financial venue in the UK and brings new rules of engagement.

- **Independence and the final ordeal**: Arya has been tested and her company gains traction. She earns a seat at the table with her brand story and its implicit values.

- **Completion and fulfilment**: She overcomes the barriers of age and gender, becomes a shining example of diversity and inclusion, and is a beacon for STEM girls. Her story is widely publicised.

Consider:

- Does your story have a rags to riches element?

- Carry out a SWOT to show how you will use your Strengths and Opportunities to rise above the Weaknesses and Threats *(more in Chapter 7)*.

- Start thinking about your brand promise following Workfront guidelines.

Coaching Questions for

My Brand story

- How do I identify the gap in the market to position our offering?

- How do I meet the criteria for my company to adhere to statutory regulations? For example, if you are a coaching company, you would belong to a body that regulates your practice, has a code of ethics and provides accredited CPD.

- What challenges do I have in terms of age, gender, diversity and experience? How do I overcome this?

- How do I write the values inherent in our brand story to match the emotional and rational needs of our consumers?

To sum up, we looked at brand positioning, a brand promise and what a successful brand looks like. Next, we meet a champion who shows us the psychology of branding and why it's really all in the mind.

CHAPTER FOUR

THE CHAMPION

The PE teacher blew the whistle to signal the end of the game. There were whoops of joy as the lads celebrated their final goal. They high fived and called out as they headed indoors to change before the next lesson. All except Alex Babatunde. He got off the bench and trailed behind them. His asthma was so bad that his teachers feared he would become ill during physical activity. Since they were unequipped to deal with it, Alex sat out every PE lesson. Being relegated to the benches meant that he also missed the camaraderie and fun of his mates. It left him feeling miserable and isolated.

When Alex turned fifteen, he took matters into his own hands. He decided that asthma was not going to rule his life. He was going to conquer this monstrous illness and all the negativity it brought. He formed the tagline: 'Accept No Limitations'. He spoke to the head of year and requested a pass to leave the school premises during PE. He had spotted a gym down the road and started training there. Alex began at a slow pace and if he felt a tightness in his chest, he rested. At the gym, he didn't feel alone; he just enjoyed the solitude.

DREAM STAGE

During the school break, he went to New York and stayed with his cousin. His cousin's boyfriend came in from work and Alex took one look at him and decided asthma or not - he wanted to bulk up to look like him - strong, with rippling muscles. On his return home, he started training at health clubs until he moved to a bodybuilding gym. He met professional bodybuilders who had competed. He earned their respect with his dedication to his training and they took him under their wing. Alex changed his entire lifestyle - trained, ate well and absorbed everything he could from the high-profile figures at the gyms. He started training twice a day. Every morning before breakfast, he did cardio, runs, cycles, stretches and meditation. Then he hit the gym. He believed that overcoming asthma and preparing to be a champion wasn't just physical preparation. Meditation enables him to plan things, clear his head and make sure that he is doing the things he should be doing. He never wakes and looks at his phone because this means that he loses control over his day and is reactive rather than proactive.

Alex's discipline, drive and desire to succeed became his trademark and he started being noticed in the bodybuilding world. The guys in the gym called him Big Gunz (after those bulging biceps). His mates called him Diesel, a colloquialism for being muscular with connotations of diesel engine power. He combined those nicknames to make up Big Gunz Diesel. It stuck, and the once sickly schoolboy transformed into a young man to be reckoned with. Big Gunz Diesel had instant brand story appeal on social media. His fans certainly think so. He has over 30 000 followers on Instagram alone.

However, he didn't allow any of this to get to this head and he deferred entering competitions. His first goal was to get his degree. He enrolled at Queen Mary University of London for a BSc in business management. He didn't know it then, but it was a means to an end. It was to serve him when he started his company as a lifestyle and fitness coach years later with the uncompromising mission 'Kill Your Excuses'.

His degree helped him learn marketing principles, economics, writing and public speaking. He also learnt time management, critical thinking, and how to be consistent. He mixed with a lot of different people and believed that, in a sense, university itself prepares you with life skills; it's almost like the whole world in one place. When he started working, he learnt to transfer those skills and to build on them. He used his bodybuilding background and sought opportunities on how to build a business from what started out as a hobby. He intended to enter the corporate world but couldn't resist the pull of lifestyle and fitness coaching. He kept getting requests from people asking if he would be their personal trainer. At first, he refused. Then he realised that if people were asking for this service, they must think that he was worthy of doing this role. He went back and studied and qualified to be a personal trainer. He believes that sometimes in life things just happen. He was chasing one path and another one opened up.

Nightmare stage

After lifting his heavyweight business degree Alex started competing professionally. He earned bodybuilding titles, was featured in magazines and got sponsors behind him. Then the nightmare of injuries began. In 2012 he hurt his hips so badly he could barely get out of a car or lift himself off a chair. He was literally flat-footed, and squatting put further stress on his hips. Later he had insoles designed to give him the much-needed arch. He used to go into the gym, but it felt like he was returning to his school days. He was sidelined and frustrated. After training for years, he thought of the sacrifices: lost time with family and friends, missed birthdays, and giving up short term gains for long term gains.

But for Alex, every day is a learning day. He used it as a period of reflection. He believes that it's like a business; there are swings and roundabouts and the pressure of financial worries as your brand grows muscle. He learnt resilience and the values underpinning his personal and business brand kicked in. He was raised by parents and grandparents who embedded the ethos of hard work, consistency and being true to oneself. This meant that he works from a place of passion. It isn't about making money. He built his startup with his vision and practically no money. He saw how training had transformed his life and wanted to give the same to his clients.

THE THRILLING ESCAPE FROM

INJURY STAGE

Like his asthma, Alex's injury spurred him to make a final escape from poor health. He analysed his training and since he couldn't do things the regular way, he did a lot of rehab work when he went to the gym. His thinking outside the box meant that he made progress without the conventional things that bodybuilders do when preparing for competitions. He grew mentally and physically and entered his first national competition and won. He became a staple name in his industry. He reflected on his branding success and believes that success is a culmination of work that you've done over time. As 2014 approached, he felt invincible; his strength, power and confidence rocketed. It was one time in his career when he just couldn't see himself failing. He was right on the money. He won the UKBFF London Championships, the IFBB USN BodyPower Championships and then became the UKBFF British Champion. His story secured him the biggest brand sponsor in the bodybuilding industry.

A Champion's Mindset

That year, Alex began to understand the power of mindset.

In a reflection of how he became a recognised brand, Alex believes that to control your mindset you have to control your environment. He changed gyms and surrounded himself with people who were really focused and had a progressive mindset. He is a firm believer in the adage that you are the sum of the five people you spend the most time with. Even if you follow them online, you need to pinpoint your role models and take what you need and leave the rest. The litmus test of this mindset is what you do when you are faced with obstacles. Do you tell yourself that you have a bad injury and can't train, or do you fight to overcome it every single day?

For a champion mindset, winning is not an end in itself. Alex felt it was great to be the British title holder, but he was more in love with the process. You win and everybody is around you. It's a moment of glory but it passes quickly. What stays with you is the journey that it took to get there. At the time of our interview, he referred to Anthony Joshua's victory a few days ago in Riyadh where he reclaimed the world heavyweight boxing titles. Alex commented that everyone would be around Joshua as the reigning champion at the moment of victory, but a week later people would have moved on and forgotten about it. This enables the champion to reflect further on the work that he did in that build up to victory.

He said that through hard work, you discover who you really are and what you are made of. Every time he competes, he goes for a period of personal growth and places himself in hard situations voluntarily. He doesn't cut corners if he wants to do something. Instead he sacrifices and works hard. He clarified: 'I have been true to myself because most times people only see me coming in and training, but that is a snapshot of my day. They don't see what I do when no one is looking. It's easy to work hard in the gym when everyone is looking at you. I hold myself accountable, to achieve what I need to, even when no one is watching.'

HOW DID HE POSITION HIMSELF IN THE HEALTH AND FITNESS ARENA?

Alex's consistency engendered trust and relationships with his clients. He said that if you are not true to yourself, your brand becomes unsustainable. However, consistency can be difficult. Sometimes going for a run is the last thing he wants to do. It gets cold and you don't want to go to the gym. But doing it irrespective of how you feel builds habits. His followers see him working hard, doing the things he says he does, and this shows them that nothing worthwhile is going to come easy. Often, we see someone who is successful, but we only see them at that moment. We don't see the moments prior which could be the work of the last ten to fifteen years. Motivation goes very quickly. You must have discipline.

His brand drew a mixture of clients: corporates who want to keep fit and healthy, athletes who compete, and a few LMA boxers and fellow fitness competitors.

To retain this brand loyalty, he tailors his service and approach to coaching for every client. Even though he's a personal trainer and coach, the first principle of his job is hospitality. He has to give his clients what they need. This means mentorship for some younger clients who want to know how to build a brand or how to market their brand themselves; others who want to be pushed, and some who want to be taught how to train. He has more women than men clients and finds that they have less ego than men and are willing to seek help when they need it. In contrast, men are reluctant to ask another man for help.

THE PSYCHOLOGY OF BRANDING —

IT'S ALL IN THE MIND

According to Baines et al[1], research shows that we make brand associations. These are made up of physical and non-physical attributes and benefits and elicit certain attitudes in the consumer's mind. This symbolic meaning that a brand gets is called the brand personality. This is a tool for marketers, that's you, marketing your company to form strong relationships with your consumers. This means that when we experience a brand, it evokes certain emotions and feelings. Think about the last time you were shopping online for a new pair of running trainers. Irrespective of your budget, you will have a long, lingering look at the brand that makes you feel as buff as the man in the advert - built, confident, smiling and probably with an equally toned, athletic girl running by his side as her sleek ponytail swishes from side to side.

Research[2] shows that consumers exert great influence on brands and brand values through online communities. The massive rise in online social networking - social commerce - turns consumers into brand ambassadors as they co-create. A brand's development correlates with the power of social media. This helps companies to build both closer customer relationships, and strong brand communities where customers enthuse over their brands. Also, online social support where there is a sharing of knowledge, experience and information, is linked to brand co-creation.

There are several examples of giant brands co-creating with their customers. In 2018, Coca-Cola[3] invited their Southeast Asian consumers to feedback on what really mattered to them. They were seeking a more digital focus to encourage co-creation.

Similarly, Lego[4] has a win-win co-creation concept where customers are given a platform to engage in the invention of products. If an idea has more than 10,000 votes, it is considered for production and the ultimate winner rakes in 1% of net sales. Lego has a two-fold gain: they receive feedback on their brand and a rich source of new ideas.

Brand Personalities

Brands are often infused with human characteristics that result in personalities.

The Brand Personality Scale[5] was developed by Aaker and has five dimensions of psychosocial meaning. These dimensions are:

Sincerity: wholesome, honest, down-to-earth

Excitement: exciting, imaginative, daring

Competence: intelligent, confident

Sophistication: charming, glamorous, smooth

Ruggedness: strong, masculine

Brand personality is crucial as it helps to build consumer loyalty:

Graham Hughes is the imaginative, daring adventurer who wants to preserve the planet.

Donald Brown is the intelligent, confident Master.

Arya Taware is the youthful badass rebel who is honest and down-to-earth.

Alex is the strong, masculine Millennial muscle who kills his excuses and expects you to do the same. Alex's brand personality reflects a man who is fit, healthy, strong, and whose only mission is to help you live your ideal life. He represents sincerity and ruggedness.

The Role of Social Media in His Brand Story

Social media is a powerful, free platform that helps you build a brand without any gatekeepers. Prior to this the formal means of marketing your brand was through radio, TV, magazines and newspapers and it was beyond the reach of many start-ups on a shoestring budget. Alex uses Instagram, Facebook and YouTube to showcase his work. He posts his training and meal plans to give back to the community. His followers can go to his page and check out his daily workout and learn from it. In a world saturated with instant gratification, filters and fakes, he shows that it takes effort to get results and if your content is of value your following grows organically, as his has done. He issued the caveat that we shouldn't use social media to sell. Instead we should give people the opportunity to judge his work. That's how he secured most of his contracts; people would DM him and say that they wanted him to be their personal trainer. He started a page and didn't know where it was going to grow. Prior to this, he didn't do social media. He just trained and focused on his work. However, sponsors asked him about social media pages and asked him to create them.

However, social media can also damage your brand. Alex comments that there are a few entrepreneurs who are supposedly doing well and pose next to flash cars in front of a big house, selling dreams that are not real. He feels the obligation to ensure that his pages are the opposite of that as he doesn't want to mislead people. Some social media pages promise to help you achieve something in thirty days when you hand over your money. But that's not how life works; nothing great is achieved in thirty days. It takes time.

To pre-empt damaging your brand, try and show what really happens on your social media pages including your ups and downs. When he was injured, people would run up to him and ask about his hip. And that's what it means to have a following. It was also good for them to learn that setbacks are part of the journey to success. A setback is not a time to quit but an opportunity to work around it and to prove yourself until you get better.

Of course, you can waste a lot of time on social media; you compare yourself with others and see what you perceive as their reality. This can lead to depression because you are constantly comparing yourself to others - what they have, who they are with, and what they are doing. He doesn't want his followers to look at him and think to themselves that he trains all the time so there must be something wrong with them. He doesn't feel motivated to train all the time. He just does it and followers know it.

What Steps does He take to Ensure that His Brand Remains Consistent?

He reflects on his practice and evaluates himself on a regular basis. When he gets home at night, he asks himself if he delivered every session giving it his all. Could he have done something better? He never takes his clients for granted. He plans carefully tailoring each session according to their needs. There is no one size fits all.

People tell him that he has the same reaction whether he wins or not. He believes that even when you win, there is still something that you did wrong and can improve on. Likewise, if your brand is successful, there are things that you could improve on. He concludes that it's not what you're good at that's going to hurt your brand, it's what you're not good at.

HIS LEGACY

We have all been blessed with certain gifts. His belief is that our gifts are not just for us to use for ourselves but to help other people. His are fitness and training and he wants to continue to use it to improve the lives of others.

WHAT'S HIS STORY?

Alex's story is one of overcoming the monster. Booker[6] shows us that there are five stages:

The Anticipation Stage: We see Alex sitting alone and forlorn, a young boy deprived of the things he loves the most, his friends and the fun of football. He feels the 'call' to confront this monster, which is his poor health.

The Dream Stage: Our hero prepares to battle asthma. He starts training, follows a strict diet and develops a winner's mindset.

Frustration and Nightmare Stage: The hero slips back into poor health. Now, following his injury, it is so bad he can't lift himself off the chair because of his hip injury.

Thrilling Escape from Death Stage: In a classic overcoming the monster the thrilling escape from death is literal. However, in our story, the hero grows to his 'full stature' and relishes the prize that he snatched from the monster. Alex's prize encompasses the process of training that results in a successful outcome, the setting up of his fitness business, his brand story showing him being true to himself, the string of titles and the sponsors that back his brand.

For Alex, the monster is two-fold. It is physical, his asthma and mental, the negativity and feeling of being excluded. He battles both to win the ultimate prize.

Consider:

- Is yours overcoming the monster story?

- How does coronavirus become the monster for every business, brand and individual?

- What are you going to be doing differently as a result of this monstrous disease?

COACHING QUESTIONS FOR

MY BRAND STORY

- How is my brand story giving consumers the means to self-express in terms of who they want to be?

- Which dimension on the Brand Personality Scale does my story brand fit in? How do I know?

- How will I pivot in my Brand Personality to retain brand loyalty during COVID-19?

- How do I pitch my brand story to my niche: gender, generation, social class and lifestyle?

- Have my competitors chosen this way of telling their story? If yes, how will I tell mine differently to make it unique?

- Which social media platforms would work best for my brand? How do I know?

- How will I use social media to co-create our brand?

- How will I manage my time between the day to day running of the business and engaging with social media followers and brand co-creation?

- How will I position my brand to meet the aftershocks of the pandemic crisis?

To sum up, we began to think of our stories with a distinct brand personality and how we co-create, particularly regarding online platforms. In the next chapter we look at another Millennial, Supergirl, who co-created her brand with both conventional and digital media.

Chapter Five

Supergirl

Madeleina Kay's mobile alarm woke her. It was Friday 24 June 2016, and the weather showed a sun-soaked weekend ahead. She patted her pillow and was about to go back to sleep when she saw the headlines. She leapt out of bed. Surely there must be some mistake? She called her parents both of whom were academics. They agreed - no one saw it coming - the UK had voted to leave the EU. As the day wore on, she began to feel a sense of responsibility for herself and her generation. Surely, they could have done more. Her disbelief (which was shared nationwide, including by Leavers and politicians) gave way to disquiet. That summer she reflected on how she could change things and she joined pro-EU campaigners.

The Call

However, the call for her political activism had been a few months back in 2015 when the cause of her friend's death was identified. He was a victim of the MH17 Ukraine plane crash[1]. They had grown up together; lived on the same street and attended the same school. His mum taught English to Madeleina's brother. It brought home how politics impacted a family's devastating loss. Here was a boy who had his whole life ahead of him, when it was cruelly and unnecessarily snatched from him. For Madeleina, it was a catalyst to be a part of the peace-making process.

She started university when she was 21. She was three years older than her peers and her staunch political beliefs and passion for the pro-UK campaign weren't shared by those around her. She felt completely disengaged when her mates came into class and talked about their night of revelry and who had puked where. In contrast, her concern was for her country and what she believed was a spiralling trajectory into political meltdown following the Brexit referendum.

Her sense of alarm heightened when she caught up with her best friend from school. She recently qualified as a junior doctor and hadn't seen the need to vote in the parliamentary elections. Madeleina felt frustrated that she couldn't persuade her friend to do this. After all, women died so that they could vote. She concluded that this apathy was the result of young people not being taught how the democratic process works. They lacked an understanding of what was at stake and the importance of participating in this democracy. Her slogan at the time was: 'Apathy is one of the greatest threats to democracy'. In her second year at university, she got to the point where she was being asked to do too much for the pro-EU campaign and couldn't carry on doing both. Something had to give. She went with her heart; she abandoned her degree in Landscape Architecture and set off to change her part of the world.

THE APPRENTICESHIP

She started campaigning and her self-styled name, art, costumes, slogans, and boldness saw her as a passionate Brit whose political and social activism could not be ignored. Madeleina's brand story evolved over the next three and a half years. Nobody taught her how to be an activist or told her what to do. She worked independently and was funded either through crowdfunding or a project that she had created. It was a learning process. But it also meant that she didn't have a brand dictated to her. Initially, she wore EU T-shirts. Then she made a blue star costume for her dog and everybody went crazy and wanted to take photographs. She thought of a way to capitalise on this and decided to design her own costume. In August 2017 she attended a boat party on the Thames where everyone was brandishing EU flags. She dressed as a pirate and made placards with the slogan: 'Proud Saboteur'.

Following this she wanted a more positive narrative; to depict herself as saving the UK from the disaster of leaving the EU. Enter the Supergirl costume with the Superman logo which was the exact shade of blue as the EU flag.

Her nickname EU Supergirl evolved when she turned up for a press conference in Brussels, where EU's Brexit negotiator Michel Barnier, and David Davis were due to speak. She won a blogging competition about an EU funded project in her home city of Sheffield, and part of the prize was the entry to this press conference. When she entered the building, she changed into her Supergirl costume. She cheekily sat in the front row, her flamboyant costume standing out in a sea of dark suits. She prominently displayed the front cover of her published book 'Theresa Maybe in Brexitland'. The cover portrayed politicians as characters in an Alice in Wonderland parody. The press was clamouring to interview her, and the conference was delayed. Madeleina was thrown out of the building. Some of the journalists followed her saying they had no right to do this, as she had a press pass and had been signed into the building. Her brand was born; she appeared on the BBC and was interviewed by several newspapers.

It gained traction and things blew up on Twitter; she started to get followers and presently has over 30 000. However, her supportive community is on Facebook. The EU Supergirl nickname stuck, and she capitalised on that; she continued to design new costumes and concepts to keep the conversation going.

From very early on, her branding was influenced by her activism. One of her critics described her content as polymathic. She took it as a compliment and agreed that she tried to connect everything and drew the links between politics, art, geography and culture. This stemmed partly from her education. When she was in Sixth Form College, she studied the International Baccalaureate - arts, science, maths and languages - where the aim is to encourage critical thinking and an appreciation for the interconnectedness of different subjects. She used this as a lens with which she saw the world and expressed this through her writing, art and music. Using her art, she drew connections and aimed to get people to see the bigger picture in terms of how culture can influence political and social change.

MATURITY

Although she strove to make it fun and cool for her audience and followers, she experienced sexism and ageism and often felt completely dismissed. Like many other female activists, she was told that she had a thirst for publicity. In contrast, from her experience, that term was never used with male activists. Instead, they were given a platform. Similarly, male activists gained greater media coverage than their counterparts. She was trolled and called a blond bimbo. She faced a huge backlash; critics didn't like her approach and style, and she was accused of self-promotion and self-interest. She said: 'Female activists and MPs politicians experience a level of abuse that is vitriolic. My last three years were marked by this'.

Madeleina was often part of a panel for conferences and debates. When she asked why there weren't more women on these panels, she was told that women were invited to participate, but no one was available.

WHAT VALUES DEFINE HER BRAND?

She believes that every individual's creative empowerment is important. When political movements, parties and organisations campaign they have a very corporate brand. They bring in professional designers to ensure everything matches and to establish official positioning. It leads to public disengagement as people are unable to see how these things relate to them. It is only when we hear these human stories, like her friend's tragic death, that we engage emotionally.

This outlook made her very emotive in her campaign branding. Her focus was not on the effects on the economy and other benchmarks used in politics. She had experiences where she tried to debate with people who disagreed with her and discredited her sources by pointing out that these facts were from the government. And they emphasised that it was not a government they trusted and termed it mere rhetoric. In her pro-EU branding, the aim was to make it cool, fun and positive. For her target audience, she wanted to engage increasingly to encourage and motivate. The European

Cultural Foundation awarded her a grant 'Democracy Needs Imagination' with the intention to let people express themselves as individuals and embrace that diversity and individuality while unifying.

POLITICAL MARMITE

Madeleina had the savvy to recognise that her brand wasn't for everyone. She terms herself political Marmite. Her approach was unconventional; she met with a lot of opposition particularly from those who had very conservative attitudes as to how politics should be done. She said: You don't influence change and you don't make change without being met with opposition. That is the whole point. You are trying to change the status quo.'

Her brand gave voice to critics who accused her of turning politics into a carnival. She cited an instance when there was a huge fallout from an event; it was decided that everyone would dress in sombre black. It resulted in limited news coverage and minimal reaction on social media. She wore her EU Supergirl costume to communicate the serious message that underpinned her values.

She was still a Gen Zer when she was bombarded by trolls on social media, particularly on Twitter. She dealt with the negativity but found rape and death threats terrifying. She continued with her art and activism. She said that the good thing about Facebook is that you can block and ban people from your page. They can't write anything further as it gets rid of them. In contrast, for Twitter, if users have replied to your tweet, the message remains on your content and can be read by everyone, even if you block them. In an ironic twist, Twitter trolling led to her music videos going viral, with some into hundreds of thousands.

She used the strategy where she took a screenshot of abuse and posted it on her Facebook page. She received support from followers who comment on the examples of the abuse, and people who approach her directly and tell her that they believed in her work and to ignore those that didn't. Following online abuse, a jewellery owner had a piece of jewellery engraved and sent it to her with a message of support.

She gained respect from this very opposition. Some Leavers shook her hand and others sent her messages saying that while they didn't agree with her politics, they admired her resilience. Others enjoyed her music and told her to keep it up.

When Britain left the EU, she didn't take it personally. However, she found the criticism from some Remainers deeply demoralising because it was personal and not about politics. They looked at her body of work, that she had dedicated her life to, and discredited it. When she travelled in Europe between events, she once had someone attack her saying that she was going on a holiday.

She has a massive profile in Germany and did interviews for all the national broadcasters who reported on her creativity, and fully embraced the EU Supergirl brand. A documentary maker who was doing a piece on Brexit examined her impact on the music industry.

In contrast, for the UK she felt that her activism and art were met with hostility and cynicism. While she didn't secure many interviews in the UK, internationally she did documentaries for Italy, Belgium, Japan, South Korea and New Zealand.

On the home front her dad who is a lecturer in business and management has been a rock. As a life-long academic he felt very strongly about Brexit and its impact on universities and academia. He supports her choices, shares her values and respects her art and music. She lives with him and has his financial support. He has also helped her campaign by acting as her accountant. Her support system extends to close friends who filmed her music videos, helped with applications for funding and edited her latest documentary.

Her greatest challenges have been practical and emotional.

Fundraising was always a factor. Madeleina's track record shows her being able to pitch her ideas. Despite her brand being unpopular with some, it stood the test with those who recognise its worth. She has been very effective at crowdfunding to cover personal living costs and different projects. Her crowdfunding skills were also used to help other people raise money for their projects, like Bollocks to Brexit where she raised over £20 000. There are those who love and respect what she does. Sometimes, hate speaks louder, but in the end love prevails. This led to her mission: 'If we were all a bit kinder to others the world would be a better place.'

She recounted how a friend told her that an insult is like a gift; you can choose to accept or refuse it. When you refuse it, it belongs to the person who gave it to you.

The emotional challenge was that it was demoralising to have people from her own side criticise her approach and remain motivated and continue to persevere in the face of this. It takes a lot of strength and she sought support from people who believe in her. She said that this is important, so you don't lose your confidence in what you're doing.

How can a Brand be used to Inform and Educate?

Madeleina won the Young European of the Year 2018, awarded by the Berlin-based Swartzkov Foundation and the EU. There were public nominations and from that open call, five nominees were interviewed in Berlin. It was the first acknowledgement of her work and her activism from an official source. Up to then, she had individuals and people at grassroots follow and support her. It was also significant in that it was a European organisation; the only funding that she received during those three years. Full-time UK activists are paid a living wage. The other funding was through the European Cultural Foundation which is based in Amsterdam. To keep her active in the UK, financial support, recognition and acknowledgement came from Europe. The award made her more European-focused and led to many more events, invitations and media interest within Europe. It helped her credibility and brand as a political activist, writer and musician. She spoke at political festivals where Michel Barnier was present. However, in the UK Maddie felt that there was little to no impact. They didn't like her pro-EU narrative.

Her art was originally presented under the brand of her dog, Alba White Wolf. He is a central character in her two children's books. She used illustrations, narrative and stories to educate and to engage. Her first book was about refugees; following the spike in hate crime against refugees and migrants after the Brexit referendum. She wrote it in aid of a refugee charity in Sheffield. This was followed by 'Thump the Orange Gorilla: At the Big World Zoo'. She wrote a book for a campaign, 'Save Our Trees'. It explained the environment and social benefit of keeping the streets clean. Her most recent publication was an information booklet: '24 reasons to remain' with visual image, facts and evidence to support the benefit of EU membership. It was crowdfunded and distributed to all grassroots groups across the UK.

Acceptance and Remedy

Madeleine fought a long and difficult battle but lost when Britain left the EU.

This young woman knows she will have to rebrand to keep her work relevant. She acknowledges with a crisp business sense that the pro-EU messaging system in the UK is dead. She intends to redirect her effort and is focusing on her book and the documentary which are the reflective outcomes of the past three years. At the time of our interview, she was also interviewed by a documentary maker who was producing a series on female activists across the world. He asked her what her next steps were. Her initial thoughts were that the Schwarzkopf Foundation funding was still to be used but she has no idea for what. If she considered university it would not be in the UK. She didn't want to invest in a future in this country and the tuition fees were 'insane'. She already has two years' worth of student debt. One of her options could be to study in Berlin or elsewhere in Europe and to learn a foreign language. She's gained a lot of skills: writing, editing, her art, music and crowdfunding. As she moves forward, these skills and her ability to rebrand will stand her in good stead.

Her brand story can be summed up by one of her role models, HRH Princess Laurentien of the Netherlands, whom she quotes: 'That is precisely the role of artists and change makers. They personify and create the space that pushes us to imagine new ideas and possibilities ...challenging the status quo to the point of being labelled naive, irrelevant...or worse, extremist. But it's their independence of mind that drives them'.

In a world where most want to follow or emulate others, Madeleina's self-styled brand is admired by many.

The power of Madeleina's brand lay in co-creation from her online and face -to-face supporters. Her fans engaged with her illustrations, books, music and on-screen presentation and in her perseverance to remain faithful to her beliefs. Her brand also evolved during a particular milieu from the moment the Brexit referendum result was announced.

Story plots depict universal themes - love and compassion, heroism, survival, suffering and judgement. The universal villain, the pandemic, gave rise to powerful brands in politics and world leaders.

When the British Chancellor of the Exchequer, Rishi Sunak, stood behind the podium in the wake of a hasty cabinet reshuffle following his predecessor's sudden resignation, he was thrust into the eye of the economic upheaval that the pandemic brought. He was untested, young, slight, but the weighty manner in which he delivered the measures he had set out, started his leadership brand story. While his plan was not without flaws, and lots more needed to be done, he hooked his listeners in the introduction to his story. For an infinitesimal moment, he made weary post-Brexit Brits forget party politics. Over the next few days, he used this kindling of trust, and built on it using the refrain: 'We will do all it takes'. This was a crisis tagline that connoted unprecedented measures for an unprecedented villain. When companies were given economic lifelines, his story moved to deepen the relationship.

To feel any empathy for Sunak's brand story, his consumers had to receive empathy themselves. There are some who would argue that he showed compassionate statesmanship. Others would scoff and dismiss this as not enough for the most vulnerable. But, in areas like politics, as we have seen in our very own Supergirl, your brand is like Marmite. Loved or hated - never indifferent.

In contrast, the actions of a few global leaders will see their people and history co-create their brand stories to reveal characters who lacked decisiveness, kindness or a clear understanding of how their actions harmed their people during the most catastrophic crisis in modern times. The pandemic narrates their roles as villains, rather than heroes. They forgot two things: Brand co-creation is a two-way street and empathy is reciprocal.

In rebranding, we take direction from legendary brands like Twitter, Instagram and Coca-Cola[2]. Twitter was originally used to search and use podcasts. When Apple stepped onto the podcast platform, Twitter turned to a micro-blogging platform. Instagram was initially an app that tracked users' check-ins and allowed users to attach photographs. When consumers showed an appreciation for the photo function, Instagram seized upon this.

Similarly, in 1985, Coca-Cola changed their time-honoured formula after customers in a blind test showed preference for it. However, it didn't look attractive so Coca- Cola reverted to the original formula.

The pandemic has brought home one certainty. Companies and their people have to adapt their offerings so that they become relevant and remain tenable. *More on how to achieve this in Chapter 7.*

WHAT'S HER STORY?

Maddie's plot resembles the bildungsroman, a coming of age story that covers the formative years of a character from childhood to maturity. Since we are writing a brand story and not a novel, we pick up from her final years of high school, where she seeks answers to life's questions and gains experience of the world during this process.

According to Littlehale[3], there are four stages in the bildungsroman:

The Call: The heroine traditionally leaves her family to gain her identity. In Madeleina's case, she left university and, although she lived with her parents, her campaigning took her to Europe on a regular basis.

The Apprenticeship: The heroine's growing maturity depends on her education. Her grounding in the Baccalaureate held her in good stead and enabled her to brand using writing, crowdfunding and art.

The new world didn't live up to her expectations. Her time at university didn't prove to be what she had expected or needed. To grow and explore her activism and art, she left. Her wider place of education, the country itself, didn't meet her expectations or want her brand.

The heroine finds their education in the end and gains maturity and identity. Her education and life experience were gained as she campaigned.

Maturity: The heroine gains maturity through psychological growth but it is hard-won. She experienced sexism and ageism and was trolled on social media.

Acceptance and Remedy: The character returns home and helps others with their newfound maturity and wisdom. She wrote books, appeared in documentaries and did interviews.

Consider:

- What are the strengths of Madeleina's brand story?

- Who is your micro-niche? Her niche was Europe, niched further to Germany. Her micro-niche was Berlin. At this point, she had her audience around the digital campfire ready for her brand story.

- Where is your brand ignored or unpopular? In life and business, we accept that our brand is not going to be met with open arms by all. Madeleina's world view wasn't favourable to Leavers. While there were admirers and respect from some, it didn't result in a purchase of her offerings. Her brand met with hostility from parties and people who held different political beliefs. To others, her brand brought a level of unpredictability and apprehension, for example, when she was thrown out of the EU press conference.

Coaching Questions for

My Brand Story

As we are in the throes of Covid-19 and looking ahead to the looming global recession:

- Which parts of my brand story are still relevant? How do I know this?

- How do I edit my brand story to meet consumers' needs?

- In my field, what is the greatest demand right now?

- How do I pivot to meet this demand?

- How do I make my present offerings relevant? Which of my offerings can be converted to online platforms?

- How do I show compassion to my employees during this time?

- Reflect on the world leaders whose brand stories I want to co-create. How do I use the lessons from them to make my brand stand out?

- What actions will I take if I have to start my story brand from scratch?

- Who do I need to share these reflections with?

- How will my company show agility in writing this new brand story?

- What's my timeline for creating a new story?

- Who will help me do this?

Keep a record of these reflections for Chapter 7.

To sum up, we looked at how a particular setting shapes your story, how a self-styled brand can be used to co-create and how a change in the local or international milieu can start a brand story. Next, we examine how needs and wants influence buying behaviour.

Chapter Six

The Hero's Journey

It was a crisp winter's morning. The type that Luke Murfitt believed was full of possibilities. But then he thought every day was a day for winning. He sat opposite a woman whose daily job was difficult and sometimes heartbreaking. She looked at the young man in front of her. He sat upright, his immaculately pressed white shirt and grey suit, together with his ready smile, took her by surprise. To say that he wasn't the usual type that walked through her door would be a very British understatement. She couldn't hold back her surprise:

Lady: You don't seem like the type of person who should be here.

Luke: I don't actually want to stay here.

Lady: What do you want to do?

Luke: I want to start a business and help the people who are walking through these doors.

Lady: Well that sounds great. You can go to the third floor where there is someone who works with entrepreneurs. But before you do, I'm curious, what business do you want to start?

Luke stood up with difficulty and shuffled over to the window. They were at a Jobcentre, overlooking Canary Wharf, the very heart of London's business district. He pointed with a trembling hand: 'You see those skyscrapers two blocks away? The owners are going to be my clients.'

He shook her hand and walked to the lifts. Naturally, he was going up.

He created his first job when he was eleven. He and a friend knocked on doors every Saturday morning asking if anyone wanted their car washed. They charged £5 per car and built a solid client base. However, when mid-winter approached, they threw water over the cars and it just froze. His company went into liquidation.

Next, he tried his hand at being a paperboy. He was too young to deliver so he was the standing boy, the person who gets the paper ready for delivery. He already had experience running a company, the car wash, so when the other boys turned up at 6.30, everything was ready for them. Gradually some of them didn't turn up and Luke got his chance to deliver and soon had his own route. With his new responsibility, he was given additional hours to stack shelves that paid the handsome sum of £1.50 an hour. He used his earnings to buy sweets which he sold at twice the price in the school playground.

Hie early success secured, Luke went on to become a pet shop boy and delivered hay and dog food to farms. Since eleven, he has only been out of work for two weeks.

While doing his A-levels he realised that he wanted to leave a footprint; he saved for a trip to Kenya. At seventeen, he set off for Africa. He lived in the orphanage, taught Maths and English and helped street children. He played the drums in church and met his wife Diana there. She came to the UK, trained as a nurse and years later was the first person to work in his company.

Luke worked in sales for a blue-chip company in London. He was diagnosed with Parkinson's and within two months was made redundant. He had to deal with a deteriorative disease and the sudden change in his finances.

To alleviate some financial burden, he was called to the Jobcentre to be put on a lifetime of benefits. He walked in dressed like a winner; no tracksuit bottoms for him. When he arrived, they didn't let him through the door but redirected him to the main entrance; the one for employees. He went to the staff entrance for his appointment. He told the lady who interviewed him that he didn't want to take the benefits. He wanted to employ others and give them hope and opportunity. Prior to that point he had four months doing research on the cleaning industry and observed that it had massive potential and was recession-proof. He looked at the figures and trends and realised that he only needed a small percentage of the 18 billion cleaning industry. He set some targets and signed up for a few remote seminars on how to run a cleaning company. Then he began to search for staff.

He saw mums on his daughter's playground and thought that at least some would want a job. They would have been out of work for a few years because of circumstance and timing. He came up with the idea of mothers and fathers back to work.

He went through his old client base in the financial services and within two weeks he secured a contract. He had four employees working 400 hours a month with a turnover of £5,000. He went onto seventy hours a day on one account. This early experience gave him a good foundation, but he wanted to have a niche and targeted new builds.

He used his story branding to shape the vision and values of his company, Integrity Cleaning. Their mission is to 'Get mothers back to work'. He redefined the cleaning industry. He saw that it was a broken industry; people cleaning rubbish and toilets. He reflected on how he could have someone take pride in cleaning a toilet and how he could get clients to respect the cleaners. He knew that it started from the top - with him. He respected them by paying them well, giving them flexible hours to fit around their childcare and being genuine. He said: 'I always look to elevate people because I don't like someone to feel uncomfortable. When you write the words opportunity is nowhere, I discovered that if I moved the w it becomes opportunity is now here.' He realised that people do not wake up one day and decide that they want to be cleaners. They were not born to be cleaners; they resort to it. If he could enable them to see that there was an opportunity to please the client, they will be helping themselves and their children. Instead of doing multiple jobs to make ends meet, they could do one well-paid job. Their name badges meant that they're not numbers but people. The company expanded in a short period of time and earned six figures within a year with a target of half a million for the second year.

We did our interview on the 39th floor; seated on trendy, colourful sofas with plump cushions that make you feel cosseted. Even the grey December sky couldn't diminish the silvery splendour of the Thames winding its way past Canary Wharf, and the giddying skyscrapers reflecting the lofty dreams of entrepreneurs like Luke, who came to make their fortunes. I mentioned that it was a dull day. He said that once we break through the clouds the sun is there. In this exclusive piece of real estate, it takes more than bravado and charm to walk in.

In fact, every day is a struggle. He wakes up to excruciating pain every morning. His back, shoulders and feet aching, and his mouth as dry as leather. He slowly unfolds himself; he is almost frozen, and the bed feels like a sheet of concrete. Eventually, he moves one arm as he battles to turn off the alarm. Then he takes the most difficult steps of his life. The steps to success. The first is gratitude for waking up. He thanks God for this. This leads to being thankful for many little things - that he can get into the bath without falling over.

THE WALK

Luke was contacted by an agency who said that they could get him new clients. He asked them if they could get a contract with Galliard, a leading property developer in London. They said they could get anyone except Galliard. They didn't accept calls and were with the same cleaners for years. For Luke the most valuable lesson he learnt working for his blue-chip company was that people that are the hardest to sell to, the gatekeepers, have not been presented with another option, so they stick to something that is out of date, inefficient or too expensive.

In our digital age, how do we contact the gatekeepers? When Integrity Cleaning was eight months old, he landed his biggest client. He looked over the window at a construction that had been going on for years. He picked up his briefcase, straightened his tie and crossed the road onto the construction site. He wasn't wearing a hi-vis jacket and entered through the vehicle entrance; 200 people shouted in his direction. Luke was breaking all the rules. He continued and asked for the person who organised the cleaning. He saw a door which said: 'Staff only', pressed the buzzer and said: 'Hi it's Luke from Integrity Cleaning'. And paused. He insists that the pause is the key. The person on the other side assumed that he was an employee and let him through.

He observed that when you are prospecting the hardest part is to get through the door. The more you get in, the easier it is to go further. Once he got onto the site, he was less likely to be challenged. As he progressed through each barrier people assumed that he had a right to be there. He entered the offices and said that he was looking for the senior person in charge of cleaning. They directed him to the upstairs floor of offices. He went up, looked for the biggest desk and chair, walked straight up to the person seated there, gave him his card, and reached out to shake his hand. It looked like they had a pre-arranged meeting:

Luke: When are we ready for the cleaning?

Man: Well your timing is very good. We have been building this for four years and in three days' time we are going to put out tenders for cleaning.

Luke: Good, what do we do?

He seized the opportunity to meet with the decision-makers regarding the tenders. Galliard was changing cleaning companies after 25 years. There were major companies who were going to put in tenders, and they were going to send him some emails for him to prequalify. Luke had never seen a tender in his life, but thought that while he was there, he should tour the building. He didn't know what the content of the emails would be, so after some quick thinking, he accidentally/on purpose left his briefcase behind. That way, when he came back to retrieve it, he could ask any questions he had about the tender process. As he drove home, he pulled over and emailed them to say that he had forgotten his bag and was going to pick it up in a couple of days (which was the day after he would have had a chance to look at their email) and added that there were some cappuccino sachets that they should feel free to enjoy.

When he went to retrieve his bag, he asked Galliard questions regarding previous tenders. He then got in touch with friends who were in the construction business and they helped him fill in all the answers to get to the next stage of the tender process. He went from a contract of £5000 to a tender for £100 000. He got through the initial stage and was called for an interview. He took it as the perfect opportunity to build on the relationship he had forged with the initial meeting, tour, questions, email, and subsequent meeting, ostensibly to retrieve the bag during the pre-qualification stage.

He got to the stage where he didn't just tell them what he could do but he made them realise that what they were looking for was right in front of them. Integrity Cleaning took pride in what they did. Other companies put in their tenders, but he had marshalled a team who took pride in what they did.

His strategic preparation together with his relationship building paid off. What he lacked in experience he researched carefully. He didn't know everything, but he knew how to find the information. He won the contract.

He believes that in a shop, the hardest part for salespeople (and we are all selling a product, service or experience) is the walk from the door to the countertop. For an entrepreneur, getting on to the site is not enough. He shared: 'When I'm walking, my only focus is that door and the very fact that my walk shows the confidence. The other person then starts to believe that you know what you are doing and prepares to listen to you.'

This cues the entrepreneur to tell but not sell:

- The entrepreneur is here to find a solution for you.

- Tell them the story. Don't go in and deliver the punchline.

- Give them the value instead of the price.

- Even after solutions are offered and trust is built, don't mention a price.

- Let the customers say what they can offer.

NAME, LOGO AND MISSION

Luke thought about how he wanted to do things in his company. He wanted to name it something that meant something to him and reflected the way he did business.

He was raised in a Christian family where they had young people in their home every night, with up to sixty on a Sunday. His faith is very important to him and he believes that life is an opportunity to serve people, especially those who experience hardship. His logo and business practice are based on this integrity.

He wants the logo, a droplet of water, to be recognised as a droplet of hope; every waterfall starts with a droplet. He set out to give hope and pride to the mothers and fathers that work for him. Some women held senior positions before motherhood but upon their return to work they are made to feel junior. Luke looks for the vulnerable in society and gives them a stepping stone to get back into work.

He said that he doesn't see himself as someone with Parkinson's. It is not a sickness or a negative factor that will hold him back. Instead, he regards it as a strength to spur him on and inspire others. To be a winner you have to face adversity; he uses it to get up rather than stop. People try to define themselves by painting a pretty picture. He is someone who gets out of a car and struggles to tie his shoelaces. He may put his jacket on backwards. He observes that he walks a bit silly too. He stands out because he can't move quickly and sometimes people think he's drunk. In the beginning, he was often late and found it humiliating. Time feels different when you have Parkinson's; you lose the ability to rush. Things become fiddly and you drop them. The smallest things become a challenge, and this leads to depression in many Parkinson's sufferers. It would have been easier to avoid people. Instead, he uses this disease as a driver. When he emailed his chief neurologist to tell him that he was a finalist for a business award, he was amazed at Luke's resilience because others deteriorate so quickly.

He recalled walking onto the Galliard site with 200 people and the site manager said: 'You look like you really know where you're going.'

And for Luke who battles the villain that is Parkinson's every day, that is the only certainty that matters.

The Jobcentre nominated him for the Entrepreneur of the Year 2019 in the UK Business Awards. They cited him as a beacon of hope and an example of a person with a winning mindset.

I stood on stage at the awards and held the envelope with the winners' names. There was a hushed silence. I read out the silver and bronze winners and then announced: 'Our gold winner is Luke Murfitt, Integrity Cleaning'.

Luke stood on his chair, raised his arms in victory and walked onto the stage. His family, friends and top team looked on with pride. They knew what it took for their hero to get there. They watched him battle the pain and defy disease every day. To every onlooker who burst into rapturous applause, they also knew that a story like Luke's is truly inspirational.

We know that a brand story carries a legacy, is values-driven and infused with the central character's actions. But what contributes to a legendary story is how the brand makes you feel. For example, how did you feel when you realised why Luke's hand trembled in our story opening?

The global pandemic shaped the brand stories of ordinary folk who contributed to the protection and saving of lives, at a risk to their own. These include medical staff, cleaners in hospitals, delivery drivers and neighbours who left groceries outside doors, amongst others. The news stories with their slogans, 'We are in this together' backed up by acts of compassion, gave rise to a brand that was born of this crisis. We are hooked onto their stories and want to co-create their irresistible offering - kindness.

Some big brands made commitments that showed empathy. The Texas Roadhouse CEO[1] Kent Taylor pledged his salary for a year towards frontline workers. Similarly, Motorpoint CEO[2] pledged to forego his salary to top up the wages of furloughed staff. His top team agreed to take salary cuts to help others in the workforce.

In contrast, there are many brands that will face irreparable damage as a result of self-interest.

According to Perreault & McCarthy[3] psychology influences consumers buying behaviour. Brands meet needs and wants. For example, the need to eat will make you go out and wait in a long line, standing two metres apart, as you wait to do your food shopping. Wants are learnt. You may need orange juice but only a particular brand will do.

They[4] add that we may have several needs. These are:

Physiological: Basic needs like food, drink, rest and sex.

Safety: Related to food, medicine and exercise.

Social: Related to love, friendship, status and esteem.

Personal: Self-esteem, a sense of accomplishment, fun and freedom.

The marketer must ascertain what needs and wants to fulfil and brand accordingly.

If we add motivation theory (which tells us that we are never satisfied) to this mix, our offerings are positioned in fertile ground. We edit our brand story accordingly, without losing the plot or being genuine.

What's His Story?

We started Luke's story in media res (Latin for in the midst of things); a narrative that opens in the middle. The setting, story and central character's thoughts are all revealed in the course of our interview.

Luke's is a comedy. According to Booker[5]:

- **The hero has a shadow cast over their world:** A period of uncertainty and frustration. When Luke hears his diagnosis, his world falls apart. This darkness brings uncertainty to the man who brought light and laughter to the orphans in Kenya.

- **The pressure of the darkness increases:** He is summoned to a Jobcentre to take benefits from the system although he has been enterprising since eleven.

- **He finds it frustrating and difficult to do little things**: Like getting dressed, getting out of bed every morning, and remaining positive against this deteriorative disease that sees many others succumb to the darkness of depression.

- **Finally, shadows are dispelled:** The situation is miraculously transformed in his world. He receives his award, and everyone shares his joy and celebrates the happy ending.

Consider

- What specific challenges relating to physical or mental health challenges am I faced with?

- What help can I access to meet these challenges?

- How do I remain positive in the face of this challenge?

- Which needs does my brand meet?

- How do I position my offering to convert these needs to wants?

- How did the pandemic stress test my brand?

- How do I edit my brand story accordingly?

- How do I avoid succumbing to mental illness during these uncertain economic times?

COACHING QUESTIONS FOR

MY BRAND STORY

- Which part of my story branding journey represents the long, difficult walk?

- What can I do to break it up into smaller steps?

- Who are the most vulnerable in my company? During the COVID-19 crisis, how can I protect them?

To sum up we looked at how psychological factors influence buying behaviour.

In the final chapter, we use the Imbue Story Branding Model and Imbue Story Brand Plan to map out where you are right now and how you can write or rewrite your narrative. We also look at the seventh way to tell your story - the memoir.

Chapter Seven

Imbuing You With All You Need, To Be All You Can Be

In 1877, a 22-year-old man got off a ship. His hazardous journey had not diminished his lean, athletic build, or the unruly black curls falling over his bronzed skin. Kartik's warm-brown eyes and megawatt smile lit his face into a beacon of hope. He looked at the emerald ocean, golden sands and blue skies, and took his nineteen-year-old bride's hand in his. She was petite, barely reaching her husband's shoulder. They had left their families to seek a better life, in a land far, far away from their life of poverty and struggle. They both smiled at each other - it was true. A land of such beauty felt like paradise. The promise of a sweet life lay before them. The only thing they had to do to enjoy this sweet life was work hard. This, they could do. Easily. Kartik was young, strong, hardworking, and determined. He would work his heart out to serve his employer in a five-year contract. His wife Vali would do the same, but she would be paid less than her husband (I'm thinking the same...we are still 216 years away from gender parity). After that, they would renew their contract, return home, or become independent workers. However, the government knew they were cheap labour, so they tried to sweeten the deal and offered them land when their contract expired. Another passenger disembarked, he was thirty years old. Ram's dove-grey eyes squinted against the brilliant sea, as the soft winter breeze cooled his skin. Like all the other passengers, he was dressed in filthy rags, but Ram had the gentle face of a poet.

Kartik, Vali and Ram were flogged, worked from before sunrise to after sunset, fed meagre, half-cooked rations and lived in crowded corrugated iron barracks, which provided no protection from the sweltering subtropical heat or the cold winter nights. Many of their co-workers committed suicide or deserted. These human rights violations meant that they went from indentured labourers to slaves. Of course, they had never signed up for this. Who signs up for slavery? The British government in the province of Natal, and the British in India, arranged for indentured labourers to work in the sugarcane plantations in South Africa. Indentured labourers signed their contracts with thumbprints. Right from the start, the implicit terms of trust and confidence were broken...Their children and their children's children fought for generations. They fought slavery, apartheid, bullying, victimisation, harassment. Ram's eldest son started work when he was a teenager. By the time he was forty, he owned buses and shops and was recognised for his pioneering work in sport. His youngest brother became a school principal.

Their blood runs through my veins. Kartik and Vali were Dad's grandparents. Ram Singh's eldest child was Mum's father...[1]

This extract is from my memoir Kindness, Kale & Kettlebells: A journey to self-awareness.

Mum's father is the boy I speak of in the introduction.

I was born during the apartheid era, and like all African babies, together with our mothers' sweet milk, we were inadvertently fed the insidious poison of racism. However, we were fed something else too. Kindness and courage. Like my ancestors I felt invincible when I left South Africa for the UK, seeking a sweeter life. After all, we had endured slavery and racism. We were done with those battles, weren't we?

I was a British headteacher/school principal in 2010 when I sued my employers for race discrimination; indirect race discrimination; unlawful harassment and victimisation. Two years into the case, I believed that my employers, like the British government in South Africa in 1877, had broken the implicit terms of trust and confidence in our contract. I added the claims of constructive unfair dismissal and discriminatory dismissal. This extract discusses this:

'In 2012, 135 years after their arrival in South Africa, history repeated itself - my British employers broke our contract. I was not going to turn a blind eye to my ancestor's spilt blood. After all, I wasn't raised by a village. No, I had been fed the kindness and courage of two continents.'[2]

The case was settled in 2013. After seeking therapy for depression, anxiety and PTSD, I started Imbue. It was a coaching and training company as this is what I had spent over twenty years doing. I had taught people from five to fifty as a teacher and lecturer. Since I had top leadership experience, I was able to do an executive coaching course that enabled me to work with C-suite clients.

'I decided to write a book. I made a good start and completed a few chapters. After a few weeks, I woke up one morning and felt very little enthusiasm to continue. I was distressed and wondered why I felt this way. All I had been experiencing lately was a sense of ennui, almost as if I had donned a Potteresque invisible cloak. I discarded it. My focus was sharpened, and I ceased to flit between ideas, wondering what was missing from my life. Then the realisation came - I needed to tell my own story before I could tell the story of another.'[3]

I wrote my memoir in 2018 and decided that I wanted to self-publish. Imbue diversified and became Imbue Coaching & Publishing.

One of my coaching clients read my book and encouraged me to start talking about my story. I did and added professional speaking to Imbue's offerings.

But, my life-long love for writing continued to surface. I wrote a leadership book Nail It! 7 Steps to Life & Business Mastery for Entrepreneurial Leaders.

Some C-suite executives approached me and told me that they were too busy to write and confessed that they didn't like writing. Imbue's next offering was ghostwriting.

What's My Story?

Memoirs differ from biographies. They are about a slice of your life while biographies are stories that cover your entire life. Hybrid memoirs speak of your personal life but are infused with elements of your brand story - your values, vision, taglines, and serve as learning points for other entrepreneurs.

Irrespective of the genre of your story - memoir, hybrid memoir or a short brand story, the most important thing to remember is that your story is about your reader. Yes, you are writing about yourself, but ultimately, it's about what your reader gains from your story. Remember, the art of storytelling evolved around a campfire. The skilful narrators would observe their audience and see which aspect of the story draws the most reaction - leaning in, wide eyes, fear, empathy - and use this energy as an arc for their story.

While my story is a memoir it has:

Elements of overcoming the monster: My monstrous inheritance of slavery and racism.

Quest: It is a metaphorical journey to gain self-awareness, be true to myself and forge my entrepreneurial path.

My legacy is the story itself which was written to honour my ancestors' struggle and to hand the baton to my daughters. However, my legacy is also the fervent hope that this baton is only an artefact and that my daughters and their generation; my readers; clients and listeners will never have to finish that particular race. It's done.

What must be passed on is the quest that enables every entrepreneur to tell their story and gain self-awareness. Our six heroes and heroines gained legendary status in their niche because of this branding.

As you write your story, heed the advice of de Chernatoy and dall' Olmo Riley cited by Baines[4] who claim that a brand is represented by a name, symbol, words or mark that identifies and sets a company apart from its competitors. However, brands consist of much more than this. They cite Aaker who agrees that a brand goes beyond a name or logo. It is a company's promise to the customer to deliver what it stands for with regards to functional, emotional, self-expressive and social benefits.

The following story is published on Imbue's www.imbuecoaching.com landing page:

Our Story

We started Imbue in 2015 after our Founder & Director, Sudhana Singh, changed careers. She believes that she brings not one, but two USPs: the first is the ability to fail. In spectacular fashion. The other is to get back up and rebrand. This resilience has seen her reinvent herself and our brand many times. In fact, such was the scale of her failures that she felt the need to write her memoir. And in doing so, our mission: Rewriting Your Narrative was born.

Imbue provides B2B branding, leadership coaching, and content strategy. Our rich leadership experience grounded in business, HR, education, coaching, mentoring and psychology, means that we enable our clients to position their brands strategically as they meet with change. Imbue delivers coaching that focuses on entrepreneurial leadership. Because we all know that our brands are constantly stress-tested.

Our Vision

Shaping leaders, driving results has seen our clients report greater confidence, more use of emotionally intelligent language and behaviours, and enhanced fulfilment in their lives. This is all good. We know that there is more to this though, don't we? Results. Making a difference. Living with authenticity.

Take another look at Imbue's logo. It is a blue arrow. Reaching for the sky? To the nth degree – and then beyond. At Imbue, clients know that there are higher realms waiting out there for them. We help them identify those goals and how to get there in a specified time frame.

You will also see that the arrow is curved. Exactly like those curve balls that are thrown at our clients every so often.

As leadership and branding experts, that is exactly what we are here to do – elicit your best as you position yourself to catch that curveball. And in this instance, we speak as experts because we have caught a few ourselves. These experiences certainly shaped us. We learnt even more humility; developed a greater sense of empathy; rewrote our personal vision; found our true north and made a brand promise to continue Imbuing you with all you need to be all you can be.

Our values and promise remain constant as we weather tumultuous times. We all know that COVID-19 has changed our lives and work forever. As global economies plunge and businesses shift to survive, and then regroup, remember our twin USPs. We hit rock-bottom. Many times. But we know how to get back up again. Imbue is poised; ready to help you rebrand as you co-create our new normal.

And, above all, especially during this unprecedented era, we want to dare you to Live Like a Legend.

IMBUE STORY BRAND MODEL (ISBM)

One of the requirements for my postgraduate degree was a Social Psychology research project. I chose to look at the correlation between self-disclosure and intimacy (emotional, physical, communication) in marriage. The respondents were postgraduate students from my university aged between twenty and thirty and who lived near me. As I plotted the graph that showed a direct correlation between self-disclosure and intimacy, I found that irrespective of any factor - economic, length of the marriage, age of respondents - self-disclosure always resulted in greater intimacy and more successful relationships.

During the writing of my memoir, I felt humiliated in some places and hesitated to share these chapters. But then the onion model of Social Penetration Theory reminded me that the greater the level of self-disclosure, the better the communication and relationship with my reader.[5]

I drew inspiration from this onion model to form the Imbue Story Brand Model (ISBM). This offering shows how to use self-disclosure in your story to brand and build a relationship based on trust and brand loyalty.

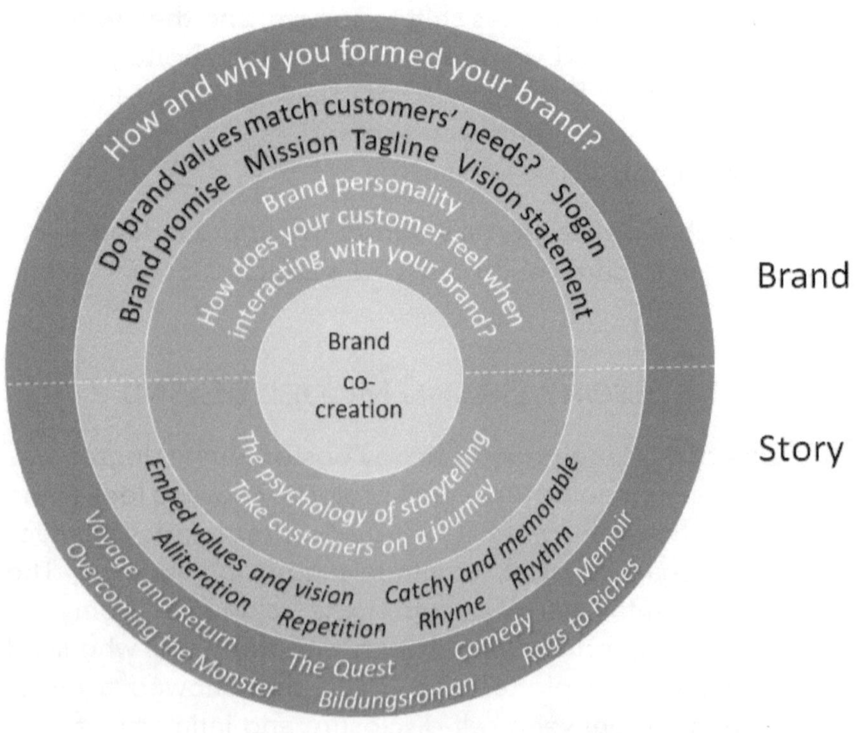

Imbue Story Brand Model (ISBM)

THE ISBN LAYERS REPRESENT THE FOLLOWING:

The first layer, which is the outermost layer, is the most superficial or general - showing why and how you started your company. One cold morning, Coco Chanel[6] pulled out an old jersey and fashioned it into a dress. She received many compliments and that day her clothing line was born. Her skillset came from the nuns who taught her how to sew when she lived in an orphanage after her mum's death. The plot has begun, and you are invited on the journey.

The next layer enables you to introduce your offering. Here the product, service or experience is referred to using language that engages the customer. Taglines, brand promises, slogans, mission, vision statements and logos draw them and build on the introduction in the first layer. Disney's tagline[7] 'The happiest place on Earth' and their slogans over time, 'I'm going to Disneyland' and 'Where dreams come true' are simple lines that are easily understood and recognised by their little consumers who have the power to open their parents' wallets. Catchy taglines and slogans are simple and have alliteration, repetition, rhyme and rhythm. Sky's is short, simple and alliterative - 'Believe in Better'.

The deepening of the relationship between you and your customer takes place within the next layer. Here the Brand Personality emerges. How does it make your customer feel when they interact with your brand? How do you use the psychology of storytelling to take them on a journey from which they return with a change in attitude? How do you keep them after interacting within the first two layers? Consumers enjoy the vicarious thrill of the story.

The innermost layer is the heart of your relationship. In fact, it has progressed to a stage where consumers care so deeply, they want to declare their love for your brand from every rooftop. They take photos when using your offerings and show it to their followers; write reviews for your book and say that it impacted them to such an extent that their call to action was to set up a WhatsApp group; recommend your offerings to others and want to be seen with you or your brand. This sweet spot of your story branding is brand co-creation. You may have started off as the central character, but your consumer has morphed from an onlooker or sidekick to a starring role in your story. When Manchester City FC[8] wanted to improve their fans' web and mobile experience, they refreshed their brand by using focus groups, surveys, user tests and prototype designs.

The aim of the ISBM is to have your customer at the heart of your brand story.

To tell a compelling story, you need an awareness of yourself and your company. The SWOT provides this.

SWOT

Strengths	Weaknesses
Opportunities	Threats

Imbue Story Branding Plan (ISBP)

While COVID-19 calls for crisis management and a shift in brand positioning, this shouldn't be a time for panicked or knee-jerk reactions. Entrepreneurial leadership enables you to maintain brand value and retain loyal consumers. Many organisations have come up with novel ways to tackle pandemic-induced problems. The good news is that you're not alone. No one was prepared for this crisis. However, it led to entrepreneurial decisions. For example, the NHS Nightingale with a 4000-bed capacity was built in nine days.

As stock markets plunge, big business collapses and unemployment soars, there is no benchmark for the scale of this crisis. However, there are some positives:

- Companies could collaborate and/or amalgamate to keep afloat.
- Opportunities to diversify offerings, for example, Ford and GM are set to produce ventilators, respirators and face masks.[6]
- We live in a digital era, unlike the time of the Depression and World War. Schools, business and governance pivoted online.
- Digital media empowers and gives a voice to ordinary people so that they feel part of the decision-making process and call out selfish behaviour on the part of any organisation, no matter its size or power.
- It enables people to keep in touch and support one another. We socially isolate but we are not alone.

The Imbue Story Branding Plan (ISBP) sets out the main objective and micro-steps on rebranding.

Strategy (What)	Rationale for action (Why)	Toolkit (How)	Resources & Budget (Who)	Timeline (When)	Story Marketing (Where)
Rewrite present story	COVID-19 made our offering irrelevant or displaced our brand value	Use ISBM and results from SWOT	Board, top team, partners, coach, mentors	Start in May 2020. Share story by the end of the month.	In-house newsletter/email/ publication Website Email list Social media Publishing platforms like Amazon
Carry out SWOT	Check relevance of our offering	Video conferencing	Top team and representatives from each department	Immediately	Website and email lists to keep customers in the loop
How can we adapt our offering, brand positioning	Set out the strategy for short-term - mission	Do market research with loyal customers			Email lists, social media Surveys using Apps
Which offerings do we keep?	COVID-19 had little or no impact. E.g. if you offer content marketing strategy.	Use this Opportunity or Strength to reassure customers.			Email to stakeholders and customers
Develop new offering	Offering is no longer tenable?	What was your most successful brand? Why did it work? What learning can you take from this?	How will you meet cost? Look at the government bailout for your company. Consult your accountant		Use every digital platform to market new offerings. Show customers how your brand will meet their needs and wants.
Stress test your offering	Can it withstand the unprecedented stressors?	Training Coaching Offer free samples to escalate demand.			Build its resilience into your brand story.

Imbue Story Brand Plan (ISBP)

We've been on this branding journey for seven chapters now. We've gotten to know each other as we shared our stories. Boss Branding is an offering that is a combination of my life and work experience as a coach, writer, leader and educator. I invite you to co-create my and Imbue's next chapter.

Consider:

- Is the memoir for you? Do you have a story that had a tremendous impact on the course of your life or that of others? Which slice of your life will you write about?
- Do you have a particular set of skills or knowledge that calls for a hybrid memoir?

Coaching Questions for

My Brand story

- How will I take readers on my journey and have them return with a change in attitude towards my offering?

We analysed the plot points of seven brand stories as the most powerful marketing tool as we seek to connect with one another. Branding theory and brand marketing practices are embedded in these stories. These include the psychology of brand storytelling; how brands help customers; brand positioning; brand promise, and what makes a successful brand. The use of taglines, slogans and mission illustrate brand value. Branding theories draw from psychology and reflects brand personalities. As you position your offering during the COVID-19 climate, the ability to lead in entrepreneurial ways is important.

A toolkit of the SWOT, ISBP and ISBM provides scaffolding as you plan and write your brand story.

As the final story draws to an end and you leave the fireside to return to your lives and companies, remember to deliver on every promise you made to your customers in your brand story.

Write it from your heart.

Live Like a Legend!

Acknowledgments

I have a confession to make; when I listened to Graham Hughes's story, I was jealous. He has travelled everywhere. He is also a natural storyteller with quintessential British humour and the most down-to-earth manner. This belies the tenacity and daredevil courage that was needed in bucket loads to become a Guinness World Record holder. His interview lasted just over two hours and was in three parts because he was travelling (naturally) and the more I heard it, the more I began to wonder how I would do it justice. Graham's brand sees him at the forefront; a pioneer who advocates how we can protect the planet against climate change and global warming.

I'm still grappling with the fact that Donald Brown is not only the Masters' fastest man in the world for his age category, but also an award-winning sculptor whose clientele includes Hollywood A-listers. Our interview setting was in the vicinity of the Queen Elizabeth Olympic Park, a fitting venue to talk about how this Master hurdled his way to gold. But his humility and social conscience see him impacting global peace efforts using the powerful levers of art and sport.

There are times when we encounter people who are leading a quiet revolution in the way we do business. Arya Taware is one such woman. Her boss branding has turned the construction and FinTech industry on its head. Her humility and willingness to arrange our interview around my timelines reminded me of why winning brands are really nothing more than 'how you make people feel'.

During my initial call to Alex Babatunde, I was reminded of the old kernel that branding starts from the first few seconds of interaction. We were arranging a time to meet for an interview. He said that he could move everything around, but for picking up his three-year-old daughter from the nursery. His sincerity and family values served to brand him as a bodybuilding champion with heart.

Madeleina Kay's quest to change the landscape of Britain was only outmatched by the time she sacrificed for her cause. She was preparing a documentary, had interviews with the media and was planning a trip to Brussels, but this 25-year-old generously set aside time on a Friday night to get the interview done.

Luke Murfitt had the winning story at the awards I judged. I interviewed him in Canary Wharf, London, overlooking the very skyscrapers that his company cleans. He has the ability to laugh at himself and very quickly makes you forget that he is struggling with Parkinson's. His story has all the elements of a traditional tale - an entrepreneurial, clean-cut hero, a villain in the form of Parkinson's disease, and the legendary theme of helping the most vulnerable in society.

In addition, I am grateful to:

Jayren Sooful, Director & Founder of UAI Technologies Johannesburg, for designing the Imbue Story Brand Model (ISBM).

The branding and marketing experts who reviewed the book.

Alan Howard of Headshot Photography London for the book jacket photograph.

The Wishing Shelf for book jacket design, editing and advice on all aspects of the book.

My readers, clients and other well-wishers who continue to co-write my brand story.

Glossary

Bunny chow – A South African fast food dish made from a hollowed-out loaf of white bread filled with vegetarian or meat curry. Originally created by Indian South Africans.

FinTech - Financial Technology

IFBB USN - The International Federation of Bodybuilding and Fitness

Jobcentre – A UK government office dispensing information and advice on job openings. It also administers benefits to unemployed citizens.

Local Authority – British local government

Proof of Concept – Evidence from a pilot project or experiment showing that a service, product design or concept is feasible.

Prototype – A first version or test of an idea, design, process, product, service, technology or creative work.

Scouser - A person from Liverpool, England.

Sixth Form – The final two years at a British school for students between the ages of 16 and 18 who are preparing for A or AS level exams.

STEM - Science, Technology, Engineering and Mathematics

Stress Test – A way of determining how well a financial institution will cope in an economic crisis.

UKBFF - United Kingdom Bodybuilding and Fitness Federation

USN - Ultimate Sports Nutrition

NOTES AND SOURCES

INTRODUCTION

1. Interbrand (2020) Best Global Brands 2019 Rankings [online]. Available from: https://www.interbrand.com/best-brands/best-global-brands/2019/ranking/ [17th March 2020]

CHAPTER 1

1. Hughes, G. (2017) Man of the World. Ohio: Atbosh Media Ltd.

2. Baines, P., Fill, C. & Rosengren, S. (2017) Marketing. Oxford: Oxford University Press.

3. Baines, P., Fill, C. & Rosengren, S. (2017) Marketing. Oxford: Oxford University Press.

4. Schreiner, C., Appel, M., Isberner, M. & Richter, T. (2018) Argument Strength and the Persuasiveness of Stories. Discourse Processes. 55(4), 371-386.

5. Booker, C. (2004) The Seven Basic Plots. London: Bloomsbury.

6. Booker, C. (2004) The Seven Basic Plots. London: Bloomsbury.

CHAPTER 2

1. Baines, P., Fill, C. & Rosengren, S. (2017) Marketing. Oxford: Oxford University Press.

2. Ziady, H. (2020) The world's biggest food company is now making vegan sausages [online]. CNN Business. Available from: https://edition.cnn.com/2020/01/17/ business/nestle-plant-based-sausage/index.html [Accessed 27th March 2020]

3. Wu, A. (2019) The Story Behind Tesla's Success (TSLA) [online]. Investopedia. Available from: https://www.investopedia.com/articles/personal-finance/061915/story-behind-teslas-success.asp [Accessed 27th March 2020]

4. Winton, J. (2011) Is Your Tagline the Same as Your Brand Promise? [online]. Mission Minded. Available from: https://mission-minded.com/is-your-tagline-the-same-as-your-brand-promise/ [Accessed 27th March 2020]

5. Prater, M. (2020) Why Your Brand Needs a Tagline and Slogan in 2020 [online]. Brand Folder. Available from: https://brandfolder.com/blog/tagline-slogan-vision-mission [Accessed 8th April 2020].

6. Tottenham Hotspur (2018) Audi and Spurs: A winning partnership [online]. Available from: https://www.tottenhamhotspur.com/news/2018/august/audi-and-spurs-a-winning-partnership/ [Accessed on 30th March 2020]

7. Tottenham Hotspur (2018) Audi and Spurs: A winning partnership [online]. Available from: https://www.tottenhamhotspur.com/news/2018/august/audi-and-spurs-a-winning-partnership/ [Accessed on 30th March 2020]

8. Booker, C. (2004) The Seven Basic Plots. London: Bloomsbury.

CHAPTER 3

1. Chernatony, L. & Riley, F.D. (1998) Defining a "Brand": Beyond the Literature with Experts' Interpretations. Journal of Marketing Management. 14(5), 417-443.

2. Baines, P., Fill, C. & Rosengren, S. (2017) Marketing. Oxford: Oxford University Press.

3. Baines, P., Fill, C. & Rosengren, S. (2017) Marketing. Oxford: Oxford University Press

4. Gardner, J. (2013) Brand-Thinking: A Shift from Tactical to Relational [online]. Branding Mag. Available from: https://www.brandingmag.com/2013/08/23/ brand-thinking-a-shift-from-tactical-to-relational/ [Accessed 27th March 2020]

5. Finkle, C. (2019) Brand Promise [online]. Brand Marketing Blog. Available from: https://brandmarketingblog.com/articles/branding-definitions/brand-promise/ [Accessed 2nd March 2020]

6. Workfront (2018) The 5 Building Blocks of an Effective Brand Promise [online]. Available from: https://www.workfront.com/blog/the-5-building-blocks-of-an-effective-brand-promise [Accessed 2nd March 2020]

7. Booker, C. (2004) The Seven Basic Plots. London: Bloomsbury.

CHAPTER 4

1. Baines, P., Fill, C. & Rosengren, S. (2017) Marketing. Oxford: Oxford University Press.

2. Wang, Y. & Hajli, M. (2014) Co-Creation in Branding Through Social Commerce: The Role of Social Support, Relationship Quality and Privacy Concerns [online]. SSRN. Available from: https://papers.ssrn.com/sol3/ papers.cfm?abstract_id=2449127 [Accessed 27th March 2020]

3. Warsia, N. (2018) Re-imaging the Coca-Cola experience by going digital first [online]. Digital Market. Available from: http://www.digitalmarket.asia/re-imagining-coca-cola-experience-going-digital-first/ [Accessed 27th March 2020]

4. Gilliland, N. (2018) Lego to BMW: How brands have used co-creation to earn consumer trust [online]. Econsultancy. Available from: https://econsultancy. com/lego-to-bmw-how-brands-have-used-co-creation-to-earn-consumer-trust/ [Accessed 27th March 2020]

5. Baines, P., Fill, C. & Rosengren, S. (2017) Marketing. Oxford: Oxford University Press.

6. Booker, C. (2004) The Seven Basic Plots. London: Bloomsbury.

CHAPTER 5

1. BBC (2020) MH17 Ukraine plane crash: What we know [online]. Available from: https://www.bbc.co.uk/news/world-europe-28357880 [Accessed 10th March 2020]

2. The Growth Revolution (2020) 10 World famous brands that only became successful after changing direction [online]. Available from: https://thegrowth revolution.com/10-famous-products-that-had-to-change-to-become-successful/ [Accessed 31st March 2020]

3. Littlehale, K. (2020) Bildungsroman Novels [online]. Available from: https://www.storyboardthat. com/articles/e/bildungsroman-novels [17th March 2020]

CHAPTER 6

1. Ruiz, M. (2020) Texas Roadhouse CEO foregoes salary for 1 year to pay workers amid coronavirus reports [online]. Fox News. Available from: https://www.foxnews.com/us/texas-roadhouse-ceo-foregoes-pay-workers-coronavirus [Accessed 1st April 2020].

2. Sharpe, T. (2020) Motorpoint CEO gives up wage to top-up income of 'furloughed' staff [online]. AM Online. Available from: https://www.am-online.com/independents/news/2020/03/30/motorpoint-ceo-gives-up-wage-to-top-up-income-of-furloughed-staff [Accessed 10th March 2020]

3. Perreault, W.D. & McCarthy, J. (1997) Essentials of Marketing. Chicago: Irwin.

4. Perreault, W.D. & McCarthy, J. (1997) Essentials of Marketing. Chicago: Irwin.

5. Booker, C. (2004) The Seven Basic Plots. London: Bloomsbury.

CHAPTER 7

1. Singh, S. (2018) Kindness, Kale & Kettlebells: A journey to self-awareness. London: Imbue Publishing.

2. Singh, S. (2018) Kindness, Kale & Kettlebells: A journey to self-awareness. London: Imbue Publishing.

3. Singh, S. (2018) Kindness, Kale & Kettlebells: A journey to self-awareness. London: Imbue Publishing.

4. Baines, P., Fill, C. & Rosengren, S. (2017) Marketing. Oxford: Oxford University Press.

5. West, R. & Turner, L. (2007) Introducing Communication theory Analysis and Application. New York: McGraw-Hill.

6. Biography (2020) Coco Chanel Biography [online]. Available from: https://www.biography.com/fashion-designer/coco-chanel [Accessed 29th March 2020]

7. Robinson, R. (2020) 30 Companies with Famous Brand Slogans & Taglines [online]. Adobe Spark. Available from: https://blog.adobespark.com/2020/02/05/30-companies-with-famous-brand-slogans-taglines/ [Accessed 29th March 2020]

8. Milbrath, S. (2019) Co-Creation: 5 Examples of Brands Driving Customer-Centric Innovation [online]. Vision Critical. Available from: https://www.visioncritical.com/blog/5-examples-how-brands-are-using-co-creation [Accessed 29th March 2020]

www.ingramcontent.com/pod-product-compliance
Lightning Source LLC
Chambersburg PA
CBHW021328060726
47591CB00006B/1920